THE SONNETS

By WILLIAM SHAKESPEARE

Preface and Annotations by
HENRY N. HUDSON

Introduction by
CHARLES HAROLD HERFORD

The Sonnets
By William Shakespeare
Preface and Annotations by Henry N. Hudson
Introduction by Charles Harold Herford

Print ISBN 13: 978-1-4209-5557-6
eBook ISBN 13: 978-1-4209-5558-3

This edition copyright © 2017. Digireads.com Publishing.

Cover Image: a detail of an illustration by Charles Robinson from "The songs and sonnets of William Shakespeare", London, Duckworth & co., 1915.

Please visit *www.digireads.com*

CONTENTS

SONNETS

Introduction

Shakespeare's Sonnets were first printed in 1609, with the following title-page:—
SHAKE-SPEARE'S—SONNETS. | Neuer before Imprinted. | AT LONDON. | BY *G. Eld* for *T. T.*, and are | to be solde by *William Aspley.* | 1609. |

In some copies 'John Wright, dwelling at Christchurch gate,' is named as the seller.

At the end of the Sonnets was printed A LOVER'S COMPLAINT.

In 1640 the great majority of the Sonnets were reissued (together with some of the poems from *The Passionate Pilgrim* and *A Lover's Complaint* and some pieces not by Shakespeare) in a volume entitled:—
POEMS: | WRITTEN | BY | WIL. SHAKE-SPEARE Gent. | Printed at *London* by *Tho. Cotes*, and are to be sold by *John Benson*, dwelling in | St *Dunstans* Churchyard. 1640.

The order of the Sonnets is here arbitrary, and Nos. XVIII, XIX, XLIII, LVI, LXXV, LXXVI, XCVI, and CXXVI are omitted. The eighteenth-century editors, Gildon (1710), Sewell (1725), Ewing (1771), and Evans (1775), followed this order.

Of definite chronological data we have two only.

(i) *The Passionate Pilgrim*, published in 1599, contained, with trifling variations, the two Sonnets CXXXVIII and CXLIV,

(ii) Meres, in 1598, mentioned, as already familiar and celebrated, Shakespeare's 'sugred sonnets among his private friends.'

Love's Labour's Lost, published in the same year, contained two Sonnets, and *Romeo and Juliet* (pr. 1597) a third; none of these, however, appear in the collection of 1609.

All that can be inferred from these facts is that Shakespeare had written some sonnets by 1598.

Attempts have been made to supplement this very inadequate conclusion by inferences, more or less plausible, from particular passages. Thus (1) CVII 5, 'The mortal moon hath her eclipse endured,' has been variously understood of the peace of Vervins in 1598, of the Essex plot against Elizabeth (1601), and of Elizabeth's death. Mr. Lee's parallels from her obituary literature leave little doubt that the last was the event referred to. (2) The reiterated declaration in CII f. that 'three years' had passed since the beginning of the friendship, and thus of the sonnet sequence itself, if we may accept it literally, in so far narrows the limits of possible date. (3) An allusion in the *Avisa* of Henry Willobie (1594) to a familiar friend of his, one 'W. S.,' as having 'not long before tried the courtesy of a like passion' [*i.e.* suffered from the cruelty of a mistress], and 'now newly recovered of the like infection,' has been thought to refer to Shakespeare and to the love-adventure which some of them reflect. This passage would go far to show that the passion of the sonnets sprang more from Shakespeare's imagination than from his heart, had we any definite ground for identifying 'W. S.' with Shakespeare. But it is impossible to draw any inference from grounds so slight. (5) Numerous affinities of style and thought connect the Sonnets with the Poems and with a group of plays which can be approximately dated. From 15 90-97, Shakespeare's dramatic writing was influenced by lyric ideals of style, predominating in *Love's Labour's Lost*, the *Midsummer-Nights Dream*, and *Romeo and Juliet.* From 1597, this style rapidly gave way to the more nervous and masculine speech of the later Histories and Comedies. There is a strong presumption that the Sonnets—Shakespeare's consummate achievement in lyric poetry—belong to this period of pronounced lyrical energies. In particular, Sonnets I-XXVI have unmistakable affinities of style and motive with the *Venus and Adonis.*

The first publisher of the Sonnets printed them, as such collections were commonly printed, in a continuous series, without any outward marks either of connexion or of division. Some critics have supposed the sequence to be wholly arbitrary. But it is clear that there is at least one definite division, at CXXVI. All the Sonnets up to that point are addressed to a youth. Of the remaining twenty-eight, seventeen are addressed to the poet's mistress, and the majority of the rest utter his bitter reflections upon the fatuous passion she has inspired. The fundamental situation is put with the utmost trenchancy in CXLIV:—

> Two loves I have of comfort and despair,
> Which like two spirits do suggest me still:
> The better angel is a man right fair,
> The worser spirit a woman colour'd ill.

The love of the 'worser spirit' is a love of despair, and the Sonnets inspired by it have a tragic intensity absent from the most despondent of the Sonnets of 'comfort.' The poet loves in spite of his best self, and his intellect is divorced from his love instead of, as in the finest of the earlier series, seeing with love's eyes and finding in it and through it 'the meaning of all things that are.' Within a smaller compass it strikes more various notes. As it stands it seems devoid of continuity. Its fitful arrangement and spasmodic movement may be partly due to disturbance of the original order; as where two half-playful pieces, CXXVIII and CXXX, are interrupted by the stern solemnity of CXXIX; but it seems rather to reflect the tumult of impulses evoked by a passion in its nature anarchical.

In the first series, on the other hand, a certain continuity is unmistakable, and it is of a kind not at all suggestive of the editorial hand.[1] The Sonnets form a succession of groups, some of which were probably continuous poetic epistles, closed with an 'envoy' (cf. XXXII, LV, LXXV, XCVI). The order of the several groups also seems by no means arbitrary. Displacement may be here and there suspected;[2] but on the whole they form a connected sequence, passing by delicate gradations through a rich compass of emotion.

The Sonnets of the opening group (I-XIV) betray the admirer rather than the friend. Their theme accords with their less personal tone. It is not so much in the interest of 'the man right fair' as of the beauty which he 'holds in lease' (XIII) that he bids him marry and beget offspring in whom it may survive. That the wife might share his friend's heart is a thought at which his affection is not yet arrogant enough to feel any jealous pang. But if his friend rejects that mightier way of immortalising his beauty, then the poet offers his verse, and the humility of the lowly worshipper breaks suddenly into the exultation of the poet who has power to embalm the fading summer of human beauty in the eternity of art (XVIII).

At XXVII the exaltation of love begins to be touched with pain, and from this point until c we pass through a region of intricately inwoven light and gloom. At first it is only the pain of *absence*; a theme which recurs in several later groups. Here it is handled in a mood of exquisitely sensitive meditation: 'When to the sessions of sweet silent thought' (xxx). In XLIII-XLVII the emotion is less keen, the thought more artificial and ingenious; in XCVII-XCIX the sense of longing is almost overpowered by the richness and splendour of the imagery which conveys it. This striking difference in tone favours the view of many critics, that these groups represent three periods of absence. But already in XXXIII a note of sharper suffering is struck. A third person enters the drama, a woman, whose love the poet's friend has won; she happens to be the poet's mistress (XLII), but it is as friend not as lover that he feels the pang: 'That thou hast her, it is not all my grief, . . . That she hath thee, is of my wailing chief.' In LXXVIII-LXXXVI a fourth person is introduced,—a rival poet, who spends his might in celebrating 'Will,' making Shakespeare 'tongue-tied, speaking of your fame!'

To these pangs of wounded love are added other 'strains of woe' less clearly defined and more rarely touched: discontent with his humble rank and means, public resentment and ill-will (XXIX, XC); the

---

[1] Mr. Lee stands alone among recent critics of weight in disputing this. 'If the critical ingenuity,' he declares, 'which has detected a continuous thread of narrative in the order that Thorpe printed Shakespeare's Sonnets were applied to the booksellers' miscellany of Sonnets called *Diana* (1594), that volume . . . could be made to reveal the sequence of an individual lover's moods . . . quite as convincingly as Thorpe's collection' (*W. Shakespeare*, p. 96 n.). He may be invited to try.

[2] Thus the three 'Absence' Sonnets, XCVII-XCIX, betray a frank and joyous confidence hard to reconcile with the desolate 'farewell' note of the previous group and with the silence which follows.

spectacle in the world at large of wrong triumphant over virtue and wisdom, and 'captive good attending captain ill' (LXVI); the sense, quickened by his friend's brilliant adolescence, of the passing away of the glory of his own youth (LXXIII). To these complex griefs the poet of the Sonnets applies two powerful solvents—love and poetry. Sometimes the glory of the lover is uppermost, sometimes the glory of the poet; sometimes they blend. Even in its moments of bitterest disillusion, his love does not cease to be a fascination, nor the monumental phrasing of it a delight. When 'absent' he can revel like the rich man in his treasure, 'The which he will not every hour survey, For blunting the fine point of seldom pleasure' (LII). 'When in disgrace with fortune and men's eyes,' his soul sings hymns at the thought of his friend's sweet love (XXIX); when grieving for the dead, that thought restores all losses (XXX); when his friend plays him false, he can ignore the momentary 'clouding of his sun' (XXXIII), and exult in his inseparable unity with the friend who has robbed him of his love (XL, XLII). Even his friend's scorn cannot make him disloyal: 'Such is my love, to thee I so belong, That for thy right myself will bear all wrong' (LXXXVIII). Only when utterly driven from his friend's heart will his endurance break down, and then his life will give way too (XCII), unless haply he should live on in ignorance of what he has lost and glory in the beauteous habitation of vice, 'where beauty's veil doth cover every blot' (XCV).

And the poet comes in aid of the lover. The 'decrepit' poet, 'lame by fortune's dearest spite,' is yet conscious of his own 'better part'; and glories in its power as that which will perpetuate, like the perfume of dead roses, the 'truth' of the fickle friend (LIV, LV, LX, LXII, LXIII, LXV), and perpetuate himself, after death, in his friend's memory (LXXIV).

If the lover's intoxication gives the climax to the first Absence group (XXVII-XXXII), that of the poet communicates its wonderful *rallegrando* to the close of the Betrayal-group (XXXIII-LV) which follows; and in the ensuing group (LVII-LXXV), as has been seen, it is a dominant inspiration, culminating once more in the close. In the group beginning at LXXVI the poet takes cognisance of the world's opinion of his poetry, glories in its 'barren monotony,' since 'you and love are still my argument,' and scorns the 'alien pens' which owe all their eloquence to the virtues of their subject (LXIX). But in the final revulsion (LXXXVII) the literary glories of poetry are forgotten: it is no more the eternal monument of passion, only its lyric cry. The anguish of the 'Farewell! thou art too dear for my possessing' craves no marble record.

The closing Sonnets of this section leave it doubtful how we are to interpret this farewell. But it was not final, and already the three closing 'Absence' Sonnets (XCVII-XCIX)—if these are rightly placed—with their confident and even playful intimacy, spring like 'a budding morrow' in the midnight of desolation. Yet an interval of silence follows (CIV), and when the poet takes up the pen again, reminiscence of the old intimacy is mingled with pleas for forgiveness. Clearly there was something more than silence to forgive. Courtly chidings of his truant Muse (C, CI), ingenious excuses for neglect (CII), are succeeded by fresh assurances that though he has 'ranged' from his 'home of love' (CIX),'gone here and there and made myself a motley to the view' (CX), and 'hoisted sail to all the winds which should transport me farthest from your sight' (CXVII), he is yet not 'false of heart' (CIX). The Siren limbecks 'foul as hell' which had beguiled him had only fortified his love (CXIX). But he was guilty of offences enough, bred by the subduing bias of his profession (CXI), and magnified by 'vulgar scandal' (CXII, CXXI), and only the friend's love and pity fills the impression stamped by that brand upon his brow. This and some other Sonnets resume thoughts already uttered in the earlier sections. The distinguishing note of this final group is the magnificent assurance of the triumph of love. The splendid 'Let me not to the marriage of true minds admit impediments' (CXVI) is the intellectual focus of the entire Sonnet series. 'Love's not Time's fool'; and as Love supersedes all mechanic records of the past (CXXII), so it makes the new births of time familiar (CXXIII) and emancipates from the caprices of Fortune (CXXIV).

The supreme poetic worth of the Sonnets makes the question of their origin in one sense idle. They are there, once for all, and their beauty is neither enhanced nor impaired, whether they reflect Shakespeare's actual experiences or body forth his dreams. But the student of Shakespeare's mind is compelled to seek a solution to this problem,—to find a *modus vivendi* between Wordsworth's confident assertion, that Shakespeare here 'unlock'd his heart,' and Browning's peremptory retort: 'Did Shakespeare? If so, the less Shakespeare he!' The discussion has hitherto tended to become a debate between two extreme views, both congenial to matter-of-fact critics of different types. The one sees in the Sonnets pure autobiography, the other a mere literary exercise. The zest of controversy has, however, generated a large amount of investigation, some of it of high value, along the lines thus suggested. Since Malone first called attention to the Sonnets, in 1780, the attempt to identify the actors in the personal history they suggest has never flagged, and it has been pursued with unsurpassed eagerness during the last two years. Mr. Lee, who has taken a leading part in working out the personal background of the Sonnets, nevertheless allows personal influence an extremely limited share in their production, and his comparative survey of the methods and *motifs* of the Elizabethan sonneteers is the most important contribution yet made to the view that Shakespeare's sonnets originated in 'the exacting conventions of the sonneteering contagion, and not in his personal experiences or emotions.'

Both these extreme views, if they do not imply a certain bluntness of literary perception, have at least tended to concentrate attention upon matters foreign to literature, or to what is most vital in literature. But it is necessary to summarise the results.

The most negative criticism of the Sonnets admits that they were addressed to a real youth. For the most part it admits also the reality of the 'rival poet' and the 'dark lady,' and of the intrigue in which all four are represented as involved. In the first controversy, the supporters of the claims of William Herbert, Earl of Pembroke, appeared, until recently, to hold the field. Their case rested largely upon highly equivocal arguments,—the dedication 'To Mr. W. H.,' and the play (in cxxxv) upon the name 'Will'; fortified by some facts of undoubted significance, such as Herbert's known unwillingness to marry, and his intrigue with a woman who demonstrably had relations with Shakespeare's company.[3] But Mary Fitton's history and person have proved to be in very imperfect accord with the characteristics of the 'dark lady' of the Sonnets; her 'raven-black' hair was brown, her 'eyes so suited'[4] were grey. Such discrepancies are not fatal to the identification, but they give it no support, and Pembroke's connexion with Mrs. Fitton in no way mitigates the grave chronological difficulty involved in his claim. For Herbert, who was born in 1580, came to London, as a youth of eighteen, in the spring of 1598. If he was the person addressed, Shakespeare had made his acquaintance, won his friendship, produced some at least of his 'sugred Sonnets,' and Francis Meres had read them, written of them, and passed his book through the tedious processes of Elizabethan publication, within six months of that date. The suggestion that the Sonnets thus celebrated belonged to a different series, of which, in spite of Shakespeare's fame, no syllable ever became, or has become, known, could only be justified by direct evidence that Herbert was the friend addressed.

The rival claims of Henry Wriothesley, Earl of Southampton, have been kept in the background by the extravagance of some of his advocates, as well as by apparent discrepancies, which a more minute scrutiny of his history does much to remove. Seven years older than Pembroke (he was born October 6, 1573), he was already, when Shakespeare made his acquaintance in 1592, among the most brilliant figures at court. The words in which Shakespeare dedicated to him, in 1593 and 1594, the *Venus and Adonis* and the *Lucrece*, show that their acquaintance swiftly ripened into intimate friendship. Many other men of letters enjoyed his patronage. Nash (1594), Gervase Markham (1595), Florio (1596) dedicated works to him; Barnabe Barnes (1593)

---

[3] Kempe, in 1600, dedicated to her his *Nine dates wonder*.
[4] Sonnet CXXVII. The text, by an obvious blunder, refers to her 'eyes' twice: probably 'hairs' is to be restored.

and Gabriel Harvey (1593) addressed him in enthusiastic Sonnets. His portraits attest his personal beauty.[5] He resisted the wish of his mother and his guardian (Burleigh) to find him a wife (1593). Two years later he fell in love with Elizabeth Vernon, a Maid of Honour, secretly married her in 1598, and incurred thereby the Queen's lasting resentment. During the autumn of 1599, in disgrace at court, he is recorded to have passed his time 'merely in going to plays every day.' He joined in Essex's conspiracy, and it was Shakespeare's *Richard II.* that they chose as a provocative on the eve of action. Narrowly escaping his friend's fate, he passed the rest of the reign in prison. His prompt release by James was welcomed with a jubilant outburst of song from his wide literary *clientele.*

What we know of Southampton's career sufficiently satisfies the meagre biographical data of the Sonnets; but its acceptance leaves many problems still unsolved. The dark lady remains as mysterious as before. The determination of date is not altogether clear. The first Sonnets must be referred to the days when 'our love was new' (CII), that is, to 1593-95. This is one of a group of retrospective Sonnets, some of which, such as civ, must be placed three years later, others possibly later still. Mr. Lee holds that CVII celebrates Southampton's release from prison on the accession of James.[6]

The identification of the 'rival poet' remains, in spite of some promising suggestions, a matter of surmise only. That there was, strictly speaking, more than one is shown by the repeated use of the plural ('every alien pen hath got my use,' LXXVIII). Some are referred to with disdain,—as owing all their merit to the inspiration of their patron's eyes,—

> Thine eyes that taught the dumb on high to sing
> And heavy ignorance aloft to fly.—LXXVIII.

But one is singled out for lofty though embittered praise, a 'better

---

[5] Miss Stopes has even detected the 'buds of marjoram' (XCIX 7) in the curling tips of his long locks.

[6] The Herbertists explain this of the revolt of Essex in1601; some recent Southamptonists think of the Spanish perils which ended with the peace of Vervins, 1598. Miss C. C. Stopes has recently sought to connect it with the fears entertained for Elizabeth in her climacteric year, 1596 (*Athen.* Mar. 26, 1898). She adduces a MS. letter of Camden's in the Cotton collection (*Julius Cæsar,* iii. f. 64), which, though it does not prove her case, is of some interest. Camden wrote to Cotton on March 15, 1596: 'I know you are (as all have been) in a melancholy and pensive cogitation.' The Queen had suffered from 'a sleepless, indisposition,' with 'an inflammation from the breast upward,' 'and her mind altogether averted from medicine in this her climacterical year did more than terrify us all, especially the last Friday in the morning,' so that the lords of the council, in great alarm, took hurried measures to defend the court and the treasure, arrested a number of gentlemen known to be 'hunger-starved for innovations,' and shipped 'all the vagrants here about' to the Low Countries.

spirit,' before whose 'precious phrase by all the Muses filed'
Shakespeare's 'tongue-tied Muse in manners holds her still' (LXXXV).
Mr. Lee has suggested that among the throng was Barnabe Barnes, a
young poet who in the early nineties was promising more in poetry than
he was destined to perform. But it is hard to believe that Barnes was the
recipient of the high compliments of LXXXVI, particularly if, as Mr. Lee
thinks, he was the 'dumb' and 'heavy' poet of LXXVIII.[7] On the other
hand, the attempt of Professor Minto to identify the eulogised rival with
Chapman, the 'proud full sail of whose great verse' seems to be so
felicitously described, is met by the difficulty, serious to a
Southamptonist, that Chapman had not produced any notably 'great
verse' before 1598.

Nor can much weight be attached (cf. Lee, p. 135) to Minto's
parallel between Chapman's sententious imagery—it is hardly more—
about the supernatural 'familiars' who inspired or deluded him,—'an
unthrifty angel that deludes my simple fancy,'—and Shakespeare's jest
at 'that affable familiar ghost who nightly gulls him with intelligence.'
Yet there were elements in both Shakespeare and Chapman which
qualified the one to play Hotspur to the other's Glendower, and the
hypothesis is at least well invented. Mr. Wyndham, finally, makes a
resolute attempt to fix Shakespeare's eulogy upon Michael Drayton
(Poems *of Shakespeare*, 255 f.).

It remains to add a single word upon the opposite class of
investigations which have established the existence in the Sonnets of a
large element of thought and *motif* which belonged as common topics
to Elizabethan sonneteering at large. Mr. Lee has thrown a flood of
light upon the contemporary sonnet in England and in France. But his
conclusions in regard to Shakespeare, notwithstanding the admirable
learning which he has arrayed in their support, are vitiated by the
assumption that a thought or a phrase which can be paralleled from
contemporary literature is thereby proved to have no relation to the
poet's 'experience or emotions,' but only to his propensities of
imitation or rivalry, of judicious posing or calculated flattery.[8] These
are not the moods in which even a Shakespeare produces the supreme
poetry of the Sonnets. Of all so-called 'imitative' elements in them

---

[7] Mr. Lee sees an allusion in these lines to Barnes' sonnet to Southampton, wherein
he celebrated Southampton's 'eyes' ('Those heavenly lamps which give the Muses light')
and begged him—

> To view my Muse with your judicial sight;
> Whom, when time shall have taught by flight to rise,
> Shall to thy virtues of much worth aspire.

[8] 'The sole biographical inference deducible from the Sonnets is that at one time in
his career Shakespeare disdained no weapon of flattery in an endeavour to monopolise
the bountiful patronage of a young man of rank' (Lee, p. 159).

there is not one which he has not touched to finer issues and steeped in the exquisite and unmistakable hues of his own mind. The process of creation which they suggest is one equally distinct from a simple rendering of personal experience and the borrowed expression of the experience of others—a process in which a definite individual experience of emotion and passion forms a persistent undercurrent of all poetic activities, a vital *point de repaire* to which thought and imagination continually recur, and which determines the direction of their boldest and seemingly most independent flights. The world of the Sonnets is always a little aloof from actualities, but never remote from them; the personalities of friend and mistress are continually suggested, but we never catch their profile, or realise any single definite trait or act of theirs. The little tokens of favour, the smile, the passing word, the vital moments of intercourse which are enshrined in the lyric monuments of Petrarch, have apparently no part in Shakespeare's. On the other hand, the metaphysical ideas, the Platonic commonplaces of Elizabethan thought, are wrought into intimate union with the concrete emotions of friendship and love. No philosophic system, Platonic or other, is to be gathered from the Sonnets, any more than from the dramas. The personal relation draws all the intellectual material to its own focus and impresses upon it its own bias and complexion. Thus, as Mr. Wyndham has pointed out,[9] the Elizabethan theory of beauty as expounded by Hoby in his translation of Castiglione's *Il Cortegiano* and by Spenser in the *Hymnes*, conceived it as 'an influence of the heavenly bountifulness' reflected in earthly things. But for Shakespeare the Friend's beauty becomes itself the very archetypal pattern and substance of which all beautiful things are but shadows. His is—

Beauty's pattern to succeeding men.—XIX.

And where the Platonist thought holds its own successfully, it is with the sacrifice of every tittle of technical phraseology. That Love triumphs over Time, for instance, was a commonplace of the schools; but how intensely Shakespearean is the expression of it:

Love's not Time's fool.

---

[9] *Poems of W. Shakespeare*, CXXII.

And how intimately the thought appears inwoven with his experience
and conviction, in the magnificent defiance of the closing lines:

> If this be error and upon me proved,
> I never writ, nor no man ever loved.—CXVI.

CHARLES HAROLD HERFORD

1900.

Preface

"Book called Shakespeare's Sonnets" was entered in the
Stationers' register by Thomas Thorpe, on the 20th of May, 1609, and
published the same year. Thorpe was somewhat eminent in his line of
business, and his edition of the Sonnets was preluded with a book-
seller's dedication, very quaint and affected both in the language and in
the manner of printing; the printing being in small capitals, with a
period after each word, and the wording thus: "To the only begetter of
these ensuing Sonnets, Mr. W. H , all happiness, and that eternity
promised by our ever-living Poet, wisheth the well-wishing adventurer
in setting forth, T. T."

There was no other edition of the Sonnets till 1640, when they
were republished by Thomas Cotes, but in a totally different order from
that of 1609, being cut, seemingly at random, into seventy-four little
poems, with a quaint heading to each, and with parts of *The Passionate
Pilgrim* interspersed. This edition is not regarded as of any authority,
save as showing that within twenty-four years after the Poet's death the
Sonnets were so far from being thought to have that unity of cause, or
purpose, or occasion, which has since been attributed to them, as to be
set forth under an arrangement quite incompatible with any such idea.

In the preface to *Venus and Adonis* I quote a passage from the
Palladis Tamia of Francis Meres, which speaks of the Poet's "sugared
Sonnets among his private friends." This ascertains that a portion, at
least, of the Sonnets were written, and well known in private circles,
before 1598. It naturally infers, also, that they were written on divers
occasions and for divers persons, some of them being intended,
perhaps, as personal compliments, and others merely as exercises of
fancy. Copies of them were most likely multiplied, to some extent, in
manuscript; since this would naturally follow both from their intrinsic
excellence, and from the favour with which the mention of them by
Meres shows them to have been regarded. Probably the author added to
the number from time to time after 1598; and, as he grew in public
distinction and private acquaintance, there would almost needs have
been a growing ambition or curiosity among his friends and admirers,

to have each as large a collection of these little treasures as they could. What more natural or likely than that, among those to whom, in this course of private circulation, they became known, there should be some one person or more who took pride and pleasure in making or procuring transcripts of as many as he could hear of, and thus getting together, if possible, a full set of them?

Two of the Sonnets, the 138th and the 144th, were printed, with some variations, as a part of *The Passionate Pilgrim* in 1599. In the same publication, which was doubtless made ignorantly and without authority, there are also several others, which, if really Shakespeare's, have as much right to a place among the Sonnets as many that are already there. At all events, the fact of those two being thus detached and appearing by themselves may be fairly held to argue a good deal as to the manner in which the Sonnets were probably written and circulated.

We have seen that Thorpe calls the "Mr. W. H.," to whom he dedicates his edition, "the only begetter of these ensuing Sonnets." The word *begetter* has been commonly understood as meaning the person who was the cause or occasion of the Sonnets being written, and to whom they were originally addressed. The taking of the word in this sense has caused a great deal of controversy, and exercised a vast amount of critical ingenuity, in endeavouring to trace a thread of continuity through the whole series, and to discover the person who had the somewhat equivocal honour of *begetting* or inspiring them. And such, no doubt, is the natural and proper sense of the word; but what it might mean in the mouth of one so anxious, apparently, to speak out of the common way, is a question not so easily settled. That the Sonnets could not, in this sense, have been *all* begotten by *one* person, has to be admitted; for, if it be certain that some of them were addressed to a man, it is equally certain that others were addressed to a woman. But the word *begetter* is found to have been sometimes used in the sense of *obtainer* or *procurer*; and such is the only sense which, in Thorpe's affected language, it will bear, consistently with the internal evidence of the Sonnets themselves. As for the theories, therefore, which have mainly grown from taking Thorp's *only begetter* to mean *only inspirer*, I set them all aside as being irrelevant to the subject. I have no doubt, that "the only begetter of these ensuing Sonnets" was simply the person who made or procured transcripts of them, and got them all together, either for his own use or for publication, and to whom Thorpe was indebted for his copy of them.

But Thorpe wishes to his Mr. W. H. "that eternity promised by our ever-living Poet." Promised by the Poet to whom? To "Mr. W. H." or to himself, or to some one else? For aught appears to the contrary, it may be to either one, or perhaps two, of these; for in some of the Sonnets, as the 18th and 19th, the Poet promises an eternity of youth and fame both to his verse and to the person he is addressing. Here may be the proper place for remarking that the 20th has the line, "A man in hue all hues in his controlling." Here the original prints hues in Italic type and with a capital, *Hews*, just as *Will* is printed in the 135th and the 136th, where the author is evidently playing upon his own name. Tyrwhitt conjectured that a play was intended on the name of *Hughes*, and that one W. Hughes may have been the "Mr. W. H." of Thorpe's dedication, and the person addressed in the Sonnets. It is indeed possible that the 2oth, and perhaps some others, may have been addressed to a personal friend of the Poets so named, who was the *procurer* of the whole series for publication: I say *possible*, and that seems the most that can be said about it.

Great effort has been made, to find in the Sonnets some deeper or other meaning than meets the ear, and to fix upon them, generally, a personal and autobiographical character. It must indeed be owned that there is in several of them an earnestness of tone, and in some few a subdued pathos, which strongly argues them to be expressions of the Poet's real feelings respecting himself, his condition, and the person or persons addressed. This is particularly the case with a series of ten, beginning with the 1o9th. Something the same may be said of the 23d, 25th, and 26th, where we find a striking resemblance to some expressions used in the dedications of the *Venus and Adonis* and of the *Lucrece*. But, as to the greater part of the Sonnets, I have long been growing more and more convinced that they were intended mainly as exercises of fancy, cast in a form of personal address, and perhaps mingling an element of personal interest or allusion, merely as a matter of art; whatever there is of personal in them being thus kept subordinate and incidental to poetical beauty and effect. For instance, in the 138th, than which few have more appearance of being autobiographical, the Poet speaks of himself as being old, and says his "days are past the best"; yet this was printed in 1599, when he was but thirty-five. Surely, in this case, his reason for using such language must have been, that it suited his purpose as a poet, not that it was true of his age as a man.

Much light is thrown on these remarkable effusions by the general style of sonneteering then in vogue, as exemplified in the Sonnets of Spenser, Drayton, and Daniel. In these too, though unquestionably designed mainly as studies or specimens of art, the authors, while speaking in the form of a personal address, and as if revealing their own actual thoughts and inward history, are continually using language and imagery that clearly had not and could not have any truth or fitness save in reference to their purpose as poets. In proportion to the genius and art of the men, these Sonnets have, as much as Shakespeare's, the appearance of being autobiographical, and of disclosing the true personal sentiments and history of the authors; except, as already mentioned, in some few cases where Wordsworth is probably right in saying of the Sonnet, that "with this key Shakespeare unlock'd his heart." For, indeed, it was a common fashion of the time, in sonnet-writing, for authors to speak in an ideal or imaginary character as if it were their real one, and to attribute to themselves certain thoughts and feelings, merely because it suited their purpose, and was a part of their art as poets, so to do. And this, I make no doubt, is the true key to the mystery which has puzzled so many critics in the Sonnets of Shakespeare. In writing Sonnets, be naturally fell into the current style of the age; only, by how much he surpassed the others in dramatic power, by so much was he better able to express ideal sentiments as if they were his own, and to pass out of himself into the characters he had imagined or assumed.

Taking this view of the matter, I of course do not search after any thread or principle of continuity running through the whole series of Sonnets, or any considerable portion of them. I hold them to have been strictly fragmentary in conception and execution, written at divers times and from various motives; addressed sometimes, perhaps, to actual persons, sometimes to ideal; and, for the most part, weaving together the real and the imaginary sentiments of the author, as would best serve the end of poetical beauty and effect. In fine, I think he wrote them mainly as an artist, not as a man, though as an artist acting more or less upon the incidents and suggestions of his actual experience. Doubtless, too, in divers cases, several of them have a special unity and coherence among themselves, being run together in continuous sets or clusters, and forming separate poems. This avoids the endless tissue of conflicting theories that has gathered about them, and also clears up the perplexity and confusion which one cannot but feel while reading them under an idea or persuasion of their being a continuous whole.

I give the Sonnets in the same order and arrangement which they have in the original edition, believing that this ought not to be interfered with, until the question shall be better settled as to the order in which they should be printed. Nevertheless, I am far from thinking this order to be the right one: on the contrary, I hold it to be in many particulars altogether disordered. It seems quite evident that there is much misplacement and confusion among them; sometimes those being scattered here and there, which belong together, sometimes one set being broken by the thrusting-in of a detached member or portion of another set. For instance, the three playing upon the author's name clearly ought to stand together; yet they are printed as the 135th, 136th, and 143d; the last of the trio being thus separated from the rest by the interposition of six jumbled together, apparently, all out of their proper connection in other sets. 50, again, the 127th, 131st, and 132d clearly ought to stand together, being continuous alike in the subject and in the manner of treating it. Numerous other cases of like dislocation might easily be pointed out.

Touching the merit of the Sonnets, there need not much he said. Some of them would hardly do credit to a school-boy, while many are such as it may well be held an honour even to Shakespeare to have written; there being nothing of the kind in the language approaching them, except a few of Milton's and a good many of Wordsworth's. That in these the Poet should have sometimes rendered his work excessively frigid with the euphuistic conceits and affectations of the time, is far less wonderful than the exquisite beauty, and often more than beauty, of sentiment and imagery that distinguishes a large portion of them. Many might be pointed out, which, with perfect clearness and compactness of thought, are resplendent with the highest glories of imagination; others are replete with the tenderest pathos; others, again, are compact of graceful fancy and airy elegance; while in all these styles there are specimens perfectly steeped in the melody of sounds and numbers, as if the thought were born of music, and the music interfused with its very substance. Wordsworth gives it as his opinion, that "there is no part of the writings of this Poet, where is found, in an equal compass, a greater number of exquisite feelings felicitously expressed."

HENRY N. HUDSON

1881.

Sonnets

I

From fairest creatures we desire increase,
That thereby beauty's rose might never die,
But as the riper should by time decease,
His tender heir might bear his memory:
But thou contracted to thine own bright eyes,
Feed'st thy light's flame with self-substantial fuel,
Making a famine where abundance lies,
Thy self thy foe, to thy sweet self too cruel:
Thou that art now the world's fresh ornament,
And only herald to the gaudy spring,
Within thine own bud buriest thy content,
And tender churl mak'st waste in niggarding:
   Pity the world, or else this glutton be,
   To eat the world's due, by the grave and thee.[1]

II

When forty winters shall besiege thy brow,
And dig deep trenches in thy beauty's field,
Thy youth's proud livery so gazed on now,
Will be a tatter'd weed of small worth held:
Then being asked, where all thy beauty lies,
Where all the treasure of thy lusty days;
To say, within thine own deep sunken eyes,
Were an all-eating shame, and thriftless praise.
How much more praise deserv'd thy beauty's use,
If thou couldst answer *This fair child of mine*
Shall sum my count, and make my old excuse,
Proving his beauty by succession thine!
   This were to be new made when thou art old,
   And see thy blood warm when thou feel'st it cold.

---

[1] To eat what is due to the world, by *burying thyself*, that is, by leaving no posterity, seems to be the meaning.

III

Look in thy glass and tell the face thou viewest
Now is the time that face should form another;
Whose fresh repair if now thou not renewest,
Thou dost beguile the world, unbless some mother.
For where is she so fair whose unear'd² womb
Disdains the tillage of thy husbandry?
Or who is he so fond will be the tomb,
Of his self-love to stop posterity?
Thou art thy mother's glass and she in thee
Calls back the lovely April of her prime;
So thou through windows of thine age shalt see,
Despite of wrinkles this thy golden time.
   But if thou live, remember'd not to be,
   Die single and thine image dies with thee.

IV

Unthrifty loveliness, why dost thou spend
Upon thy self thy beauty's legacy?
Nature's bequest gives nothing, but doth lend,
And being frank she lends to those are free.³
Then, beauteous niggard, why dost thou abuse
The bounteous largess given thee to give?
Profitless usurer, why dost thou use
So great a sum of sums, yet canst not live?
For having traffic with thy self alone,
Thou of thy self thy sweet self dost deceive:
Then how when nature calls thee to be gone,
What acceptable audit canst thou leave?
   Thy unused beauty must be tombed with thee,
   Which, used, lives th' executor to be.

---

² *Unear'd* is *untilled, fallow*; as to *ear* is to *plough.*—*Fond*, second line after, is *foolish*; the more usual meaning of the word in Shakespeare's time.
³ *Free* in the sense of *liberal* or *generous.*

V

Those hours, that with gentle work did frame
The lovely gaze where every eye doth dwell,
Will play the tyrants to the very same
And that unfair⁴ which fairly doth excel;
For never-resting time leads summer on
To hideous winter, and confounds him there;
Sap checked with frost, and lusty leaves quite gone,
Beauty o'er-snowed and bareness every where:
Then were not summer's distillation left,
A liquid prisoner pent in walls of glass,
Beauty's effect with beauty were bereft,
Nor it, nor no remembrance what it was:
   But flowers distill'd, though they with winter meet,
   Leese⁵ but their show; their substance still lives sweet.

VI

Then let not winter's ragged hand deface,
In thee thy summer, ere thou be distill'd:
Make sweet some vial; treasure thou some place
With beauty's treasure ere it be self-kill'd.
That use⁶ is not forbidden usury,
Which happies those that pay the willing loan;
That's for thy self to breed another thee,
Or ten times happier, be it ten for one;
Ten times thy self were happier than thou art,
If ten of thine ten times refigur'd thee:
Then what could death do if thou shouldst depart,
Leaving thee living in posterity?
   Be not self-will'd, for thou art much too fair
   To be death's conquest and make worms thine heir.

---

⁴ *Unfair* is here a verb, meaning *make unfair.*
⁵ *Leese* is an ancient form of *lose.* Not used again by Shakespeare.
⁶ *Use, usance,* and *usury,* all had the same meaning in the Poet's time.

VII

Lo! in the orient when the gracious light
Lifts up his burning head, each under eye
Doth homage to his new-appearing sight,
Serving with looks his sacred majesty;
And having climb'd the steep-up heavenly hill,
Resembling strong youth in his middle age,
Yet mortal looks adore his beauty still,
Attending on his golden pilgrimage:
But when from highmost pitch, with weary car,
Like feeble age, he reeleth from the day,
The eyes, 'fore duteous, now converted are
From his low tract, and look another way:
   So thou, thyself outgoing in thy noon:
   Unlook'd, on diest unless thou get a son.

VIII

Music to hear,[7] why hear'st thou music sadly?
Sweets with sweets war not, joy delights in joy:
Why lov'st thou that which thou receiv'st not gladly,
Or else receiv'st with pleasure thine annoy?
If the true concord of well-tuned sounds,
By unions married, do offend thine ear,
They do but sweetly chide thee, who confounds
In singleness the parts that thou shouldst bear.
Mark how one string, sweet husband to another,
Strikes each in each by mutual ordering;
Resembling sire and child and happy mother,
Who, all in one, one pleasing note do sing:
   Whose speechless song being many, seeming one,
   Sings this to thee: *Thou single wilt prove none.*

---

[7] *Thou, who art* music to hear, or *whom it is* music to hear.

IX

Is it for fear to wet a widow's eye,
That thou consum'st thy self in single life?
Ah! if thou issueless shalt hap to die,
The world will wail thee like a makeless[8] wife;
The world will be thy widow and still weep
That thou no form of thee hast left behind,
When every private widow well may keep
By children's eyes, her husband's shape in mind:
Look! what an unthrift in the world doth spend
Shifts but his[9] place, for still the world enjoys it;
But beauty's waste hath in the world an end,
And kept unused the user so destroys it.
   No love toward others in that bosom sits
   That on himself such murd'rous shame commits.

X

For shame! deny that thou bear'st love to any,
Who for thy self art so unprovident.
Grant, if thou wilt, thou art belov'd of many,
But that thou none lov'st is most evident:
For thou art so possess'd with murderous hate,
That 'gainst thy self thou stick'st not to conspire,
Seeking that beauteous roof to ruinate
Which to repair should be thy chief desire.
O! change thy thought, that I may change my mind:
Shall hate be fairer lodg'd than gentle love?
Be, as thy presence is, gracious and kind,
Or to thyself at least kind-hearted prove:
   Make thee another self for love of me,
   That beauty still may live in thine or thee.

---

[8] *Makeless* is *mateless, companionless; make* being an old word for *mate*. So in *The Faerie Queene*, iii. 11, 2:

And of faire Britomart ensample take,
That was as true in love as turtle to her *make*.

[9] *His* for *its*, referring to *what*. That which the spendthrift squanders only changes its owner, or its place of service.

XI

As fast as thou shalt wane, so fast thou grow'st,
In one of thine, from that which thou departest;
And that fresh blood which youngly thou bestow'st,
Thou mayst call thine when thou from youth convertest,
Herein lives wisdom, beauty, and increase;
Without this folly, age, and cold decay:
If all were minded so, the times should cease
And threescore year would make the world away.
Let those whom nature hath not made for store,
Harsh, featureless, and rude, barrenly perish:
Look, whom she best endow'd, she gave thee more;[10]
Which bounteous gift thou shouldst in bounty cherish:
　　She carv'd thee for her seal, and meant thereby,
　　Thou shouldst print more, not let that copy die.

XII

When I do count the clock that tells the time,
And see the brave day sunk in hideous night;
When I behold the violet past prime,
And sable curls, all silvered o'er with white;
When lofty trees I see barren of leaves,
Which erst from heat did canopy the herd,
And summer's green all girded up in sheaves,
Borne on the bier with white and bristly beard,
Then of thy beauty do I question make,
That thou among the wastes of time must go,
Since sweets and beauties do themselves forsake
And die as fast as they see others grow;
　　And nothing 'gainst Time's scythe can make defence
　　Save breed, to brave him when he takes thee hence.

---

[10] An elliptical passage, meaning, apparently, "she gave more to thee than to him whom she best endowed."

XIII

O! that you were your self; but, love,[11] you are
No longer yours, than you your self here live:
Against this coming end you should prepare,
And your sweet semblance to some other give:
So should that beauty which you hold in lease
Find no determination; then you were
Yourself again, after yourself's decease,
When your sweet issue your sweet form should bear.
Who lets so fair a house fall to decay,
Which husbandry in honour might uphold,
Against the stormy gusts of winter's day
And barren rage of death's eternal cold?
   O! none but unthrifts. Dear my love, you know,
   You had a father: let your son say so.

XIV

Not from the stars do I my judgement pluck;
And yet methinks I have astronomy,
But not to tell of good or evil luck,
Of plagues, of dearths, or seasons' quality;
Nor can I fortune to brief minutes tell,
Pointing to each his thunder, rain and wind,
Or say with princes if it shall go well
By oft predict[12] that I in heaven find:
But from thine eyes my knowledge I derive,
And constant stars in them I read such art
As truth and beauty shall together thrive,
If from thyself, to store thou wouldst convert;[13]
   Or else of thee this I prognosticate:
   Thy end is truth's and beauty's doom and date.

---

[11] *Love*, of course, for *lover*. In Shakespeare's time the language of friendship and of love was much the same. Hence *lover* was continually used where we should use *friend*. The plays have many instances in point.

[12] *Oft predict* is *frequent prediction* or *prognostication*.

[13] Meaning, apparently, "If thou wouldst turn to laying up a store from thyself for future years"; that is, change thy mind, get married, and have children to succeed thee. "*As* truth," &c., is equivalent to "*That* truth," &c.; *as* and *that* being used indifferently in the Poet's time.

XV

When I consider every thing that grows
Holds in perfection but a little moment,
That this huge stage presenteth naught but shows
Whereon the stars in secret influence comment;
When I perceive that men as plants increase,
Cheered and checked even by the self-same sky,
Vaunt in their youthful sap, at height decrease,
And wear their brave state out of memory;
Then the conceit of this inconstant stay
Sets you most rich in youth before my sight,
Where wasteful Time debateth with decay
To change your day of youth to sullied night,
   And all in war with Time for love of you,
   As he takes from you, I engraft you new.

XVI

But wherefore do not you a mightier way
Make war upon this bloody tyrant, Time?
And fortify your self in your decay
With means more blessed than my barren rhyme?
Now stand you on the top of happy hours,
And many maiden gardens, yet unset,[14]
With virtuous wish would bear you living flowers,
Much liker than your painted counterfeit:[15]
So should the lines of life that life repair[16]
Which this, Time's pencil, or my pupil pen,
Neither in inward worth nor outward fair,[17]
Can make you live your self in eyes of men.[18]
   To give away yourself, keeps yourself still,
   And you must live, drawn by your own sweet skill.

---

[14] *Unset* is *unplanted*; as we use *setting* or *setting out*, in the language of gardening.

[15] "Much *more like you* than your painted *image* or *likeness*." The Poet often has *counterfeit* in this sense.

[16] To *repair* in the sense of to *renew*. *Line of life* probably means *living line* or *lineage*; used in contrast with "painted counterfeit," an inanimate image.

[17] *Fair* for *fairness or beauty*; the concrete for the abstract.

[18] *Live* has for its object *Which*, referring to *life*. "Repair that life which nothing else can make you live, yourself," &c.

XVII

Who will believe my verse in time to come,
If it were fill'd with your most high deserts?
Though yet heaven knows it is but as a tomb
Which hides your life, and shows not half your parts.
If I could write the beauty of your eyes,
And in fresh numbers number all your graces,
The age to come would say, *This poet lies*;
Such heavenly touches ne'er touch'd earthly faces.
So should my papers, yellow'd with their age,
Be scorn'd, like old men of less truth than tongue,
And your true rights be term'd a poet's rage
And stretched metre of an antique song:
    But were some child of yours alive that time,
    You should live twice,—in it, and in my rhyme.

XVIII

Shall I compare thee to a summer's day?
Thou art more lovely and more temperate:
Rough winds do shake the darling buds of May,
And summer's lease hath all too short a date:
Sometime too hot the eye of heaven shines,
And often is his gold complexion dimm'd,
And every fair from fair sometime declines,
By chance, or nature's changing course untrimm'd:
But thy eternal summer shall not fade,
Nor lose possession of that fair thou ow'st,
Nor shall death brag thou wander'st in his shade,
When in eternal lines to time thou grow'st,
    So long as men can breathe, or eyes can see,
    So long lives this, and this gives life to thee.

XIX

Devouring Time, blunt thou the lion's paws,
And make the earth devour her own sweet brood;
Pluck the keen teeth from the fierce tiger's jaws,
And burn the long-liv'd phoenix, in her blood;
Make glad and sorry seasons as thou fleets,[19]
And do whate'er thou wilt, swift-footed Time,
To the wide world and all her fading sweets;
But I forbid thee one most heinous crime:
O! carve not with thy hours my love's fair brow,
Nor draw no lines there with thine antique pen;
Him in thy course untainted do allow
For beauty's pattern to succeeding men.
   Yet, do thy worst old Time: despite thy wrong,
   My love shall in my verse ever live young.[20]

---

[19] Here *fleets* is used for a rhyme with *sweets*, while strict grammar requires *fleetest*. So in the 8th *Sonnet:*

> They do but sweetly chide thee, who *confounds*
> In singleness the parts that thou shouldst bear.

[20] This was a customary way of speaking among the sonnet-writers of that age, and so is not to be taken as if the Poet really had any such conceit or forecast of immortality, but merely as an allowed strain of poetical license. In like sort, Spenser repeatedly speaks as if he were fully assured that his lines would both possess and confer an eternity of youth and fame. So in his 75th *Sonnet:*

> My verse your virtues rare shall eternize,
> And in the heavens write your glorious name ;
> Where, whenas death shall all the world subdue,
> Our love shall live, and later life renew.

And he has the same thought in at least two other *Sonnets.* So too in Drayton's 44th:

> To keep thee from oblivion and the grave,
> Ensuing ages yet my rhymes shall cherish,
> Where I entomb'd my better part shall save;
> And, though this earthly body fade and die,
> My name shall mount upon eternity,

A similar strain occurs in his 6th. The same promise of eternity is also met with in two of Daniel's. Thus in his 42d:

> That grace which doth more than enwoman thee
> Lives in my lines, and must eternal be.

XX

A woman's face with nature's own hand painted,
Hast thou, the master mistress of my passion;
A woman's gentle heart, but not acquainted
With shifting change, as is false women's fashion:
An eye more bright than theirs, less false in rolling,
Gilding the object whereupon it gazeth;
A man in hue all hues in his controlling,
Which steals men's eyes and women's souls amazeth.
And for a woman wert thou first created;
Till Nature, as she wrought thee, fell a-doting,
And by addition me of thee defeated,
By adding one thing to my purpose nothing.
  But since she prick'd[21] thee out for women's pleasure,
  Mine be thy love and thy love's use their treasure.

XXI

So is it not with me as with that Muse,
Stirr'd by a painted beauty to his verse,
Who heaven itself for ornament doth use
And every fair with his fair doth rehearse,
Making a couplement of proud compare'
With sun and moon, with earth and sea's rich gems,
With April's first-born flowers, and all things rare,
That heaven's air in this huge rondure[22] hems.
O! let me, true in love, but truly write,
And then believe me, my love is as fair
As any mother's child, though not so bright
As those gold candles fix'd in heaven's air:
  Let them say more that like of hearsay well;
  I will not praise that purpose not to sell.

---

[21] *Prick*, both noun and verb, was very often used for mark. Shakespeare has it repeatedly thus, So in *Julius Cæsar*, iv. 1: "These many, then, shall die; their names are *prick'd*."

[22] *Rondure* is *circle*, *bell*, or *round*.

XXII

My glass shall not persuade me I am old,
So long as youth and thou are of one date;
But when in thee time's furrows I behold,
Then look I death my days should expiate.
For all that beauty that doth cover thee,
Is but the seemly raiment of my heart,
Which in thy breast doth live, as thine in me:
How can I then be elder than thou art?
O! therefore love, be of thyself so wary
As I, not for myself, but for thee will;
Bearing thy heart, which I will keep so chary
As tender nurse her babe from faring ill.
   Presume not on thy heart when mine is slain,
   Thou gav'st me thine not to give back again.

XXIII

As an unperfect actor on the stage,
Who with his fear is put beside his part,
Or some fierce thing replete with too much rage,
Whose strength's abundance weakens his own heart;
So I, for fear of trust, forget to say
The perfect ceremony[23] of love's rite,
And in mine own love's strength seem to decay,
O'ercharg'd with burthen of mine own love's might.
O! let my looks be then the eloquence
And dumb presagers of my speaking breast,
Who plead for love, and look for recompense,
More than that tongue that more hath more express'd.
   O! learn to read what silent love hath writ:
   To hear with eyes belongs to love's fine wit.

---

[23] *Ceremony* is here used as a trisyllable, as if spelt *cer'mony*.

XXIV

Mine eye hath play'd the painter and hath steel'd[24]
Thy beauty's form in table of my heart;
My body is the frame wherein 'tis held,
And perspective it is best painter's art.
For through the painter must you see his skill,
To find where your true image pictur'd lies,
Which in my bosom's shop is hanging still,
That hath his windows glazed with thine eyes.
Now see what good turns eyes for eyes have done:
Mine eyes have drawn thy shape, and thine for me
Are windows to my breast, where-through the sun
Delights to peep, to gaze therein on thee;
    Yet eyes this cunning want to grace their art,
    They draw but what they see, know not the heart.

XXV

Let those who are in favour with their stars
Of public honour and proud titles boast,
Whilst I, whom fortune of such triumph bars
Unlook'd for joy in that I honour most.
Great princes' favourites their fair leaves spread
But as the marigold at the sun's eye,
And in themselves their pride lies buried,
For at a frown they in their glory die.
The painful warrior famoused for fight,
After a thousand victories once foil'd,
Is from the book of honour razed quite,
And all the rest forgot for which he toil'd:
    Then happy I, that love and am belov'd,
    Where I may not remove nor be remov'd.

---

[24] *Stell'd* appears to be neither more nor less than a form of *styled*, used for the rhyme; and *meaning* drawn or *depicted*.

XXVI

Lord of my love, to whom in vassalage
Thy merit hath my duty strongly knit,
To thee I send this written embassage,
To witness duty, not to show my wit:
Duty so great, which wit so poor as mine
May make seem bare, in wanting words to show it,
But that I hope some good conceit of thine
In thy soul's thought, all naked, will bestow it:
Till whatsoever star that guides my moving,
Points on me graciously with fair aspect,
And puts apparel on my tatter'd loving,
To show me worthy of thy sweet respect:
    Then may I dare to boast how I do love thee;
    Till then, not show my head where thou mayst prove me.

XXVII

Weary with toil, I haste me to my bed,
The dear repose for limbs with travel tir'd;
But then begins a journey in my head
To work my mind, when body's work's expired:
For then my thoughts—from far where I abide—
Intend[25] a zealous pilgrimage to thee,
And keep my drooping eyelids open wide,
Looking on darkness which the blind do see:
Save that my soul's imaginary[26] sight
Presents thy shadow to my sightless view,
Which, like a jewel (hung in ghastly night,[27]
Makes black night beauteous, and her old face new.
    Lo! thus, by day my limbs, by night my mind,
    For thee, and for myself, no quiet find.

---

[25] *Intend* is here used in the Latin sense of to *endeavour* or to *be intent upon*. So *intendere animum* is to *apply* or *direct the mind.*

[26] *Imaginary* for *imaginative.*

[27] So in *Romeo and Juliet*, i. 5: "Her beauty hangs upon the cheek of night like a rich jewel in an Ethiop's ear."

XXVIII

How can I then return in happy plight,
That am debarre'd the benefit of rest?
When day's oppression is not eas'd by night,
But day by night and night by day oppress'd,
And each, though enemies to either's reign,
Do in consent shake hands to torture me,
The one by toil, the other to complain
How far I toil, still farther off from thee.
I tell the day, to please him thou art bright,
And dost him grace when clouds do blot the heaven:
So flatter I the swart-complexion'd night,
When sparkling stars twire[28] not thou gild'st the even.
    But day doth daily draw my sorrows longer,
    And night doth nightly make grief's length seem stronger.

XXIX

When in disgrace with fortune and men's eyes
I all alone beweep my outcast state,
And trouble deaf heaven with my bootless cries,
And look upon myself, and curse my fate,
Wishing me like to one more rich in hope,
Featur'd like him, like him with friends possess'd,
Desiring this man's art, and that man's scope,
With what I most enjoy contented least;
Yet in these thoughts my self almost despising,
Haply I think on thee,—and then my state,
Like to the lark at break of day arising
From sullen earth, sings hymns at heaven's gate;[29]
    For thy sweet love remember'd such wealth brings
    That then I scorn to change my state with kings.

---

[28] To *twire* is to *twitter*, to *twinkle*, to *peep*. So in Fletcher's *Women Pleased*, iv. 1: "I saw the wench that *twired* and *twinkled* at thee; the wench that's new come hither, the young smug wench."

[29] It was common to speak thus of the lark soaring and singing.

XXX

When to the sessions of sweet silent thought
I summon up remembrance of things past,
I sigh the lack of many a thing I sought,
And with old woes new wail my dear time's waste:
Then can I drown an eye, unused to flow,
For precious friends hid in death's dateless night,
And weep afresh love's long since cancell'd woe,
And moan the expense of many a vanish'd sight:
Then can I grieve at grievances foregone,
And heavily from woe to woe tell o'er
The sad account of fore-bemoaned moan,
Which I new pay as if not paid before.
    But if the while I think on thee, dear friend,
    All losses are restor'd and sorrows end.

XXXI

Thy bosom is endeared with all hearts,
Which I by lacking have supposed dead;
And there reigns Love, and all Love's loving parts,
And all those friends which I thought buried.
How many a holy and obsequious[30] tearHath dear religious
love[31] stol'n from mine eye,
As interest of the dead, which now appear
But things remov'd that hidden in thee lie!
Thou art the grave where buried love doth live,
Hung with the trophies of my lovers gone,
Who all their parts of me to thee did give,
That due of many now is thine alone:
    Their images I lov'd, I view in thee,
    And thou—all they—hast all the all of me.

---

[30] *Obsequious* in the sense of *funereal*, or relating to obsequies, or mourning-rites.
[31] "*Dear-religious* love" is well explained by Walker "love *making a religion of its affections*."

XXXII

If thou survive my well-contented day,
When that churl Death my bones with dust shall cover
And shalt by fortune once more re-survey
These poor rude lines of thy deceased lover,
Compare them with the bettering[32] of the time;
And though they be outstripp'd by every pen,
Reserve[33] them for my love, not for their rhyme,
Exceeded by the height of happier men.
O! then vouchsafe me but this loving thought:
'Had my friend's Muse grown with this growing age,
A dearer birth than this his love had brought,
To march in ranks of better equipage:
  But since he died and poets better prove,
  Theirs for their style I'll read, his for his love.'

XXXIII

Full many a glorious morning have I seen
Flatter the mountain tops with sovereign eye,
Kissing with golden face the meadows green,
Gilding pale streams with heavenly alchemy;
Anon permit the basest clouds to ride
With ugly rack[34] on his celestial face,
And from the forlorn world his visage hide,
Stealing unseen to west with this disgrace:
Even so my sun one early morn did shine,
With all triumphant splendour on my brow;
But out! alack! he was but one hour mine,
The region cloud[35] hath mask'd him from me now.
  Yet him for this my love no whit disdaineth;
  Suns of the world may stain when heaven's sun staineth.

---

[32] That is, with those that *surpass* or *excel* them. The Poet often uses to *better* for to surpass.
[33] *Reserve* in the sense of *preserve*, only stronger.
[34] *Rack* was used for certain forms of cloud.
[35] "The *region* cloud" is the cloud *of the sky*. The Poet has *region* several times in this way.

XXXIV

Why didst thou promise such a beauteous day,
And make me travel forth without my cloak,
To let base clouds o'ertake me in my way,
Hiding thy bravery in their rotten smoke?
'Tis not enough that through the cloud thou break,
To dry the rain on my storm-beaten face,
For no man well of such a salve can speak,
That heals the wound, and cures not the disgrace:
Nor can thy shame give physic to my grief;
Though thou repent, yet I have still the loss:
The offender's sorrow lends but weak relief
To him that bears the strong offence's cross.
    Ah! but those tears are pearl which thy love sheds,
    And they are rich and ransom all ill deeds.

XXXV

No more be griev'd at that which thou hast done:
Roses have thorns, and silver fountains mud:
Clouds and eclipses stain both moon and sun,
And loathsome canker lives in sweetest bud.
All men make faults, and even I in this,
Authorizing thy trespass with compare,
Myself corrupting, salving thy amiss,[36]
Excusing thy sins more than thy sins are;
For to thy sensual fault I bring in sense,[37]—
Thy adverse party is thy advocate,—
And 'gainst myself a lawful plea commence:
Such civil war is in my love and hate,[38]
    That I an accessory needs must be,
    To that sweet thief which sourly robs from me.

---

[36] *Amiss* as a substantive, for *fault, misbehaviour*, or what is *done amiss*. Repeatedly so.

[37] *Sense* for *feeling*, probably. The meaning seems to be, "Though my judgment blames your fault, my feelings take your part."

[38] This is, "in my love to the *sinner* and hatred of the *sin*."

XXXVI

Let me confess that we two must be twain,
Although our undivided loves are one:
So shall those blots that do with me remain,
Without thy help, by me be borne alone.
In our two loves there is but one respect,
Though in our lives a separable[39] spite,
Which though it alter not love's sole effect,
Yet doth it steal sweet hours from love's delight.
I may not evermore acknowledge thee,
Lest my bewailed guilt should do thee shame,
Nor thou with public kindness honour me,
Unless thou take that honour from thy name:
   But do not so, I love thee in such sort,
   As thou being mine, mine is thy good report.

XXXVII

As a decrepit father takes delight
To see his active child do deeds of youth,
So I, made lame[40] by Fortune's dearest[41] spite,
Take all my comfort of thy worth and truth;
For whether beauty, birth, or wealth, or wit,
Or any of these all, or all, or more,
Entitled in thy parts[42] do crowned sit,
I make my love engrafted, to this store:
So then I am not lame, poor, nor despis'd,
Whilst that this shadow doth such substance give
That I in thy abundance am suffic'd,
And by a part of all thy glory live.
   Look what is best, that best I wish in thee:
   This wish I have; then ten times happy me!

---

[39] *Separable* for *separative*; the passive form with the active sense. So the old writers have many instances of *contemptible* for *contemptuous*.

[40] From this line, and one in the 89th Sonnet, some, Sir Walter Scott among them, have supposed the Poet to have been literally *lame*. But the expression in both cases is doubtless figurative.

[41] *Dear* was used of any thing that excited intense feeling, whether pleasant or painful.

[42] Meaning, probably, *ennobled* or *made honourable by being in thee*.

XXXVIII

How can my muse want subject to invent,
While thou dost breathe, that pour'st into my verse
Thine own sweet argument, too excellent
For every vulgar paper to rehearse?
O! give thy self the thanks, if aught in me
Worthy perusal stand against thy sight;
For who's so dumb that cannot write to thee,
When thou thy self dost give invention light?
Be thou the tenth Muse, ten times more in worth
Than those old nine which rhymers invocate;
And he that calls on thee, let him bring forth
Eternal numbers to outlive long date.
    If my slight muse do please these curious days,
    The pain be mine, but thine shall be the praise.

XXXIX

O! how thy worth with manners may I sing,
When thou art all the better part of me?
What can mine own praise to mine own self bring?
And what is't but mine own when I praise thee?
Even for this, let us divided live,
And our dear love lose name of single one,
That by this separation I may give
That due to thee which thou deserv'st alone.
O absence! what a torment wouldst thou prove,
Were it not thy sour leisure gave sweet leave,
To entertain the time with thoughts of love,—
Which time and thoughts so sweetly doth deceive;[43]
    And that thou teachest how to make one twain,
    By praising him here who doth hence remain.

---

[43] "Which *love* doth sweetly *beguile* time and thoughts."

XL

Take all my loves, my love, yea take them all;
What hast thou then more than thou hadst before?
No love, my love, that thou mayst true love call;
All mine was thine, before thou hadst this more.
Then, if for my love, thou my love receivest,
I cannot blame thee, for my love thou usest;
But yet be blam'd, if thou thy self deceivest
By wilful taste of what thyself refusest.
I do forgive thy robbery, gentle thief,
Although thou steal thee all my poverty:
And yet, love knows it is a greater grief
To bear greater wrong, than hate's known injury.
    Lascivious grace, in whom all ill well shows,
    Kill me with spites yet we must not be foes.

XLI

Those pretty wrongs that liberty commits,
When I am sometime absent from thy heart,
Thy beauty, and thy years full well befits,
For still temptation follows where thou art.
Gentle thou art, and therefore to be won,
Beauteous thou art, therefore to be assail'd;
And when a woman woos, what woman's son
Will sourly leave her till he have prevail'd?
Ay me! but yet thou might'st my seat forbear,[44]
And chide thy beauty and thy straying youth,
Who lead thee in their riot even there
Where thou art forced to break a twofold truth,—
    Hers by thy beauty tempting her to thee,
    Thine by thy beauty being false to me.

---

[44] Best explained, perhaps, from *Othello*, ii. 1: "For that I do suspect the lusty Moor hath *leap'd into my seat.*"

XLII

That thou hast her it is not all my grief,
And yet it may be said I loved her dearly;
That she hath thee is of my wailing chief,
A loss in love that touches me more nearly.
Loving offenders thus I will excuse ye:
Thou dost love her, because thou know'st I love her;
And for my sake even so doth she abuse me,
Suffering my friend for my sake to approve her.
If I lose thee, my loss is my love's gain,
And losing her, my friend hath found that loss;
Both find each other, and I lose both twain,
And both for my sake lay on me this cross:
    But here's the joy,—my friend and I are one;
    Sweet flattery!—then she loves but me alone.

XLIII

When most I wink, then do mine eyes best see,
For all the day they view things unrespected;
But when I sleep, in dreams they look on thee,
And darkly bright, are bright in dark directed.
Then thou, whose shadow shadows doth make bright,
How would thy shadow's form form happy show
To the clear day with thy much clearer light,
When to unseeing eyes thy shade shines so!
How would, I say, mine eyes be blessed made
By looking on thee in the living day,
When in dead night thy fair imperfect shade
Through heavy sleep on sightless eyes doth stay!
    All days are nights to see till I see thee,
    And nights bright days when dreams do show thee me.

XLIV

If the dull substance of my flesh were thought,
Injurious distance should not stop my way;
For then despite of space I would be brought,
From limits far remote, where thou dost stay.
No matter then although my foot did stand
Upon the farthest earth remov'd from thee;[45]
For nimble thought can jump both sea and land,
As soon as think the place where he would be.
But, ah! thought kills me that I am not thought,
To leap large lengths of miles when thou art gone,
But that so much of earth and water wrought,[46]
I must attend, time's leisure with my moan;
   Receiving naught by elements so slow
   But heavy tears, badges of either's woe.

XLV

The other two, slight air, and purging fire
Are both with thee, wherever I abide;
The first my thought, the other my desire,
These present-absent with swift motion slide.
For when these quicker elements are gone
In tender embassy of love to thee,
My life, being made of four, with two alone
Sinks down to death, oppress'd with melancholy;[47]
Until life's composition be recured[48]
By those swift messengers return'd from thee,
Who even but now come back again, assur'd,
Of thy fair health, recounting it to me:
   This told, I joy; but then no longer glad,
   I send them back again, and straight grow sad.

---

[45] The construction is, "Upon the earth farthest removed from thee."

[46] That is, being made up or composed so much of earth and water; or having so little of air and fire in my composition. Implying the old doctrine of philosophy, that all things consisted of those four elements.

[47] Here *melancholy*, as Walker says, is to be pronounced *mélanch'ly*.

[48] To *recure* is used repeatedly by the Poet for to *recover* or to *restore*.

XLVI

Mine eye and heart are at a mortal war,
How to divide the conquest of thy sight;
Mine eye my heart thy picture's sight would bar,
My heart mine eye the freedom of that right.
My heart doth plead that thou in him dost lie,—
A closet never pierc'd with crystal eyes—
But the defendant doth that plea deny,
And says in him thy fair appearance lies.
To side this title is impaneled
A quest of thoughts,[49] all tenants to the heart;
And by their verdict is determined
The clear eye's moiety[50] and the dear heart's part:
    As thus,—mine eye's due is thy outward part,
    And my heart's right, thy inward love of heart.

XLVII

Betwixt mine eye and heart a league is took,
And each doth good turns now unto the other:
When that mine eye is famish'd for a look,
Or heart in love with sighs himself doth smother,
With my love's picture then my eye doth feast,
And to the painted banquet bids my heart;
Another time mine eye is my heart's guest,
And in his thoughts of love doth share a part:
So, either by thy picture or my love,
Thy self away, art present still with me;
For thou not farther than my thoughts canst move,
And I am still with them, and they with thee;
    Or, if they sleep, thy picture in my sight
    Awakes my heart, to heart's and eye's delight.

---

[49] To *decide* this title, an *inquest* or *jury* of thoughts is impanneled.
[50] *Moiety* was any part or portion of a thing.

XLVIII

How careful was I when I took my way,
Each trifle under truest bars to thrust,
That to my use it might unused stay
From hands of falsehood, in sure wards of trust!
But thou, to whom my jewels trifles are,
Most worthy comfort, now my greatest grief,
Thou best of dearest, and mine only care,
Art left the prey of every vulgar thief.
Thee have I not lock'd up in any chest,
Save where thou art not, though I feel thou art,
Within the gentle closure of my breast,
From whence at pleasure thou mayst come and part;
    And even thence thou wilt be stol'n I fear,
    For truth proves thievish for a prize so dear.

XLIX

Against that time, if ever that time come,
When I shall see thee frown on my defects,
When as thy love hath cast his utmost sum,
Call'd to that audit by advis'd respects;[51]
Against that time when thou shalt strangely pass,
And scarcely greet me with that sun, thine eye,
When love, converted from the thing it was,
Shall reasons find of settled gravity;[52]
Against that time do I ensconce me here,
Within the knowledge of mine own desert,
And this my hand, against my self uprear,
To guard the lawful reasons on thy part:
    To leave poor me thou hast the strength of laws,
    Since why to love I can allege no cause.

---

[51] *Advised respects* is *deliberate judgment* or *consideration.*

[52] Well explained from *Julius Cæsar*, iv. 2: "When love begins to sicken and, decay, it useth an enforced ceremony."

L

How heavy do I journey on the way,
When what I seek—my weary travel's end—
Doth teach that ease and that repose to say,
Thus far the miles are measured from thy friend!
The beast that bears me, tired with my woe,
Plods dully on, to bear that weight in me,
As if by some instinct the wretch did know
His rider lov'd not speed, being made from thee:
The bloody spur cannot provoke him on,
That sometimes anger thrusts into his hide,
Which heavily he answers with a groan,
More sharp to me than spurring to his side;
     For that same groan doth put this in my mind,
     My grief lies onward, and my joy behind.

LI

Thus can my love excuse the slow offence
Of my dull bearer when from thee I speed:
From where thou art why should I haste me thence?
Till I return, of posting is no need.
O! what excuse will my poor beast then find,
When swift extremity[53] can seem but slow?
Then should I spur, though mounted on the wind,
In winged speed no motion shall I know,
Then can no horse with my desire keep pace;
Therefore desire, of perfect'st love being made,
Shall neigh—no dull flesh—in his fiery race;
But love, for love, thus shall excuse my jade,—
     'Since from thee going, he went wilful-slow,
     Towards thee I'll run, and give him leave to go.'

---

[53] *Swift extremity* is *extreme swiftness,* or the top of speed.

LII

So am I as the rich, whose blessed key,
Can bring him to his sweet up-locked treasure,
The which he will not every hour survey,
For blunting[54] the fine point of seldom pleasure.
Therefore are feasts so solemn and so rare,
Since, seldom coming in that long year set,
Like stones of worth they thinly placed are,
Or captain jewels in the carcanet.[55]
So is the time that keeps you as my chest,
Or as the wardrobe which the robe doth hide,
To make some special instant special-blest,
By new unfolding his imprison'd pride.
    Blessed are you whose worthiness gives scope,
    Being had, to triumph; being lacked, to hope.

LIII

What is your substance, whereof are you made,
That millions of strange[56] shadows on you tend?
Since every one, hath every one, one shade,
And you but one, can every shadow lend.
Describe Adonis, and the counterfeit
Is poorly imitated after you;
On Helen's cheek all art of beauty set,
And you in Grecian tires are painted new:
Speak of the spring, and foison[57] of the year,
The one doth shadow of your beauty show,
The other as your bounty doth appear;
And you in every blessed shape we know.
    In all external grace you have some part,
    But you like none, none you, for constant heart.

---

[54] *For blunting* is equivalent to *for fear of blunting*, or *lest he blunt*. The phrase occurs repeatedly.

[55] "*Captain* jewels" are *chief* or *principal* jewels. *Carcanet* is *necklace*.

[56] *Strange* in the sense of *alien* or *foreign:* shadows *not your own, not proper to you.*

[57] *Foison* is *plenty* or *abundance.*

LIV

O! how much more doth beauty beauteous seem
By that sweet ornament which truth doth give.
The rose looks fair, but fairer we it deem
For that sweet odour, which doth in it live.
The canker-blooms[58] have full as deep a dye
As the perfumed tincture of the roses.
Hang on such thorns, and play as wantonly
When summer's breath their masked buds discloses:
But, for their virtue only is their show,
They live unwoo'd, and unrespected fade;
Die to themselves. Sweet roses do not so;
Of their sweet deaths, are sweetest odours made:
   And so of you, beauteous and lovely youth,
   When that[59] shall vade, by verse distills your truth.

LV

Not marble, nor the gilded monuments
Of princes, shall outlive this powerful rhyme;
But you shall shine more bright in these contents
Than unswept stone, besmear'd with sluttish time.
When wasteful war shall statues overturn,
And broils root out the work of masonry,
Nor Mars his sword, nor war's quick fire shall burn
The living record of your memory.
'Gainst death, and all-oblivious enmity
Shall you pace forth; your praise shall still find room
Even in the eyes of all posterity
That wear this world out to the ending doom.
   So, till the judgment that yourself arise,[60]
   You live in this, and dwell in lovers' eyes.

---

[58] Canker-blooms are the blossoms of the canker-rose or dog-rose.

[59] *That* refers to *youth:* "when your youth shall fade," &c. *Vade* is the original form of *fade*; from the Latin *vado.*

[60] *Arise* is here used transitively, and is put in the plural for the rhyme, though its subject is in the singular: "Till the judgment-day that raises yourself from the dead," is the meaning—Touching the sentiment of this Sonnet, see page 30, note 20.

LVI

Sweet love, renew thy force; be it not said
Thy edge should blunter be than appetite,
Which but to-day by feeding is allay'd,
To-morrow sharpened in his former might:
So, love, be thou, although to-day thou fill
Thy hungry eyes, even till they wink with fulness,
To-morrow see again, and do not kill
The spirit of love, with a perpetual dulness.
Let this sad interim like the ocean be
Which parts the shore, where two contracted new[61]
Come daily to the banks, that when they see
Return of love, more blest may be the view;
  Or call it winter, which being full of care,
  Makes summer's welcome, thrice more wished, more rare.

LVII

Being your slave what should I do but tend,
Upon the hours, and times of your desire?
I have no precious time at all to spend;
Nor services to do, till you require.
Nor dare I chide the world-without-end hour[62]
Whilst I, my sovereign, watch the clock for you,
Nor think the bitterness of absence sour,
When you have bid your servant once adieu;
Nor dare I question with my jealous thought
Where you may be, or your affairs suppose,
But, like a sad slave, stay and think of naught
Save, where you are, how happy you make those.[63]
  So true a fool is love, that in your will,
  Though you do anything, he thinks no ill.

---

[61] Meaning, I suppose, two lovers newly engaged.
[62] The hour that, while I am watching the clock for you, seems as if it would never come to an end.
[63] "Save how happy you make those *who are* where you are."

LVIII

That god forbid, that made me first your slave,
I should in thought control your times of pleasure,
Or at your hand the account of hours to crave,
Being your vassal, bound to stay your leisure!
O! let me suffer, being at your beck,
The imprison'd absence of your liberty;[64]
And patience, tame to sufferance, bide each check,
Without accusing you of injury.
Be where you list, your charter is so strong
That you yourself may privilege your time
To what you will; to you it doth belong
Yourself to pardon of self-doing crime.
   I am to wait, though waiting so be hell,
   Not blame your pleasure be it ill or well.

LIX

If there be nothing new, but that which is
Hath been before, how are our brains beguil'd,
Which labouring for invention bear amiss
The second burthen of a former child!
O! that record could with a backward look,
Even of five hundred courses of the Sun,[65]
Show me your image in some antique book,
Since mind at first in character was done![66]
That I might see what the old world could say
To this composed wonder of your frame;
Whether we are mended, or whe'r better they,
Or whether revolution be the same.[67]
   O! sure I am the wits of former days,
   To subjects worse have given admiring praise.

---

[64] An obscure passage. The meaning seems to be, "let me suffer the imprisonment occasioned by your liberty of absence."

[65] "Courses of the Sun" are *years*. So in *Othello*, iii. 4: "A sibyl, that had number'd in the world the Sun to *course* two hundred compasses," &c.

[66] That is, since *thought* was first *expressed in writing*.

[67] Whether revolving time keeps doing the same things over and over.

LX

Like as the waves make towards the pebbled shore,
So do our minutes hasten to their end;
Each changing place with that which goes before,
In sequent toil all forwards do contend.
Nativity, once in the main of light,
Crawls to maturity, wherewith being crown'd,
Crooked eclipses 'gainst his glory fight,
And Time that gave doth now his gift confound.[68]
Time doth transfix the flourish set on youth
And delves the parallels in beauty's brow,
Feeds on the rarities of nature's truth,
And nothing stands but for his scythe to mow:
    And yet to times in hope, my verse shall stand.
    Praising thy worth, despite his cruel hand.

LXI

Is it thy will, thy image should keep open
My heavy eyelids to the weary night?
Dost thou desire my slumbers should be broken,
While shadows like to thee do mock my sight?
Is it thy spirit that thou send'st from thee
So far from home into my deeds to pry,
To find out shames and idle hours in me,
The scope and tenure of thy jealousy?
O, no! thy love, though much, is not so great:
It is my love that keeps mine eye awake:
Mine own true love that doth my rest defeat,
To play the watchman ever for thy sake:
    For thee watch I, whilst thou dost wake elsewhere,
    From me far off, with others all too near.

---

[68] To *waste*, to *consume*, were the more usual meanings of to *confound*.

LXII

Sin of self-love possesseth all mine eye
And all my soul, and all my every part;
And for this sin there is no remedy,
It is so grounded inward in my heart.
Methinks no face so gracious[69] is as mine,
No shape so true, no truth of such account;
And for myself mine own worth do define,
As I all other in all worths surmount.
But when my glass shows me myself indeed
Beated and chopp'd with tanned antiquity,
Mine own self-love quite contrary I read;
Self so self-loving were iniquity.
      'Tis thee,—myself,—that for myself I praise,
      Painting my age with beauty of thy days.

LXIII

Against my love shall be as I am now,
With Time's injurious hand crush'd and o'erworn;
When hours have drain'd his blood and fill'd his brow
With lines and wrinkles; when his youthful morn
Hath travell'd on to age's steepy night;
And all those beauties whereof now he's king
Are vanishing, or vanished out of sight,
Stealing away the treasure of his spring;
For such a time do I now fortify
Against confounding age's cruel knife,
That he shall never cut from memory
My sweet love's beauty, though my lover's life:
      His beauty shall in these black lines be seen,
      And they shall live, and he in them still green.

---

[69] *Gracious*, here, is *full of grace*, that is, *beautiful.*

LXIV

When I have seen by Time's fell hand defac'd
The rich-proud cost of outworn buried age;
When sometime lofty towers I see down-raz'd,
And brass eternal slave to mortal rage;
When I have seen the hungry ocean gain
Advantage on the kingdom of the shore,
And the firm soil win of the watery main,
Increasing store with loss, and loss with store;
When I have seen such interchange of state,
Or state itself confounded, to decay;
Ruin hath taught me thus to ruminate—
That Time will come and take my love away.
   This thought is as a death which cannot choose
   But weep to have[70] that which it fears to lose.

LXV

Since brass, nor stone, nor earth, nor boundless sea,
But sad mortality o'ersways their power,
How with this rage shall beauty hold a plea,
Whose action is no stronger than a flower?
O! how shall summer's honey breath hold out,
Against the wrackful siege of battering days,
When rocks impregnable are not so stout,
Nor gates of steel so strong but Time decays?
O fearful meditation! where, alack,
Shall Time's best jewel from Time's chest lie hid?
Or what strong hand can hold his swift foot back?
Or who his spoil of beauty can forbid?
   O! none, unless this miracle have might,
   That in black ink my love may still shine bright.

---

[70] *To have* for *at having.* The infinitive used gerundively. So in the next Sonnet but one, last line, we have *to die* for *by dying.*

LXVI

Tired with all these, for restful death I cry,—
As to behold desert a beggar born,
And needy nothing trimm'd in jollity,
And purest faith unhappily forsworn,
And gilded honour shamefully misplac'd,
And maiden virtue rudely strumpeted,
And right perfection wrongfully disgrac'd,
And strength by limping sway disabled
And art made tongue-tied by authority,
And folly—doctor-like—controlling skill,
And simple truth miscall'd simplicity,
And captive good attending captain ill;—
   Tir'd with all these, from these would I be gone,
   Save that, to die, I leave my love alone.

LXVII

Ah! wherefore with infection should he live,
And with his presence grace impiety,
That sin by him advantage should achieve,
And lace[71] itself with his society?
Why should false painting imitate his cheek,
And steel dead seeming of his living hue?
Why should poor beauty indirectly seek
Roses of shadow, since his rose is true?
Why should he live, now Nature bankrupt is,
Beggar'd of blood to blush through lively veins?
For she hath no exchequer now but his,
And proud of many, lives upon his gains.
   O! him she stores, to show what wealth she had
   In days long since, before these last so bad.

---

[71] To *lace* here means to *embellish*, to *adorn*. So in *Macbeth*, ii. 1: "His silver skin *laced* with his golden blood."

LXVIII

Thus is his cheek the map[72] of days outworn,
When beauty lived and died as flowers do now,
Before these bastard signs of fair were born,
Or durst inhabit on a living brow;
Before the golden tresses of the dead,
The right of sepulchres, were shorn away,
To live a second life on second head;
Ere beauty's dead fleece made another gay:[73]
In him those holy antique hours are seen,
Without all ornament, itself and true,
Making no summer of another's green,
Robbing no old to dress his beauty new;
    And him as for a map doth Nature store,
    To show false Art what beauty was of yore.

LXIX

Those parts of thee that the world's eye doth view
Want nothing that the thought of hearts can mend;
All tongues—the voice of souls—give thee that due,
Uttering bare truth, even so as foes commend.
Thy outward thus with outward praise is crown'd;
But those same tongues, that give thee so thine own,
In other accents do this praise confound
By seeing farther than the eye hath shown.
They look into the beauty of thy mind,
And that in guess they measure by thy deeds;
Then—churls—their thoughts, although their eyes were kind,
To thy fair flower add the rank smell of weeds:
    But why thy odour matcheth not thy show,
    The solve[74] is this, that thou dost common grow.

---

[72] Here, as usual in Shakespeare, *map* is *picture*.
[73] The Poet has several allusions to this fashion of his time, and always speaks of it in a way not very complimentary.
[74] *Solve* for *solution*; as, in the next Sonnet, *suspect* for *suspicion*.

LXX

That thou art blam'd shall not be thy defect,
For slander's mark was ever yet the fair;
The ornament of beauty is suspect,
A crow that flies in heaven's sweetest air.
So thou be good, slander doth but approve
Thy worth the greater being woo'd of time;
For canker vice the sweetest buds doth love,
And thou present'st a pure unstained prime.
Thou hast passed by the ambush of young days
Either not assail'd, or victor being charg'd;
Yet this thy praise cannot be so thy praise,
To tie up envy, evermore enlarg'd,
     If some suspect of ill mask'd not thy show,
     Then thou alone kingdoms of hearts shouldst owe.

LXXI

No longer mourn for me when I am dead
Than you shall hear the surly sullen bell
Give warning to the world that I am fled
From this vile world with vilest worms to dwell:
Nay, if you read this line, remember not
The hand that writ it, for I love you so,
That I in your sweet thoughts would be forgot,
If thinking on me then should make you woe.
O! if,—I say you look upon this verse,
When I perhaps compounded am with clay,
Do not so much as my poor name rehearse;
But let your love even with my life decay;
     Lest the wise world should look into your moan,
     And mock you with me after I am gone.

LXXII

O,—lest the world should task you to recite
What merit lived in me, that you should love
After my death,—dear love, forget me quite,
For you in me can nothing worthy prove;
Unless you would devise some virtuous lie,
To do more for me than mine own desert,
And hang more praise upon deceased I
Than niggard truth would willingly impart:
O! lest your true love may seem false in this
That you for love speak well of me untrue,
My name be buried where my body is,
And live no more to shame nor me nor you.
    For I am shamed by that which I bring forth,
    And so should you, to love things nothing worth.

LXXIII

That time of year thou mayst in me behold
When yellow leaves, or none, or few, do hang
Upon those boughs which shake against the cold,
Bare ruin'd choirs, where late the sweet birds sang.
In me thou see'st the twilight of such day
As after sunset fadeth in the west;
Which by and by black night doth take away,
Death's second self, that seals up all in rest.
In me thou see'st the glowing of such fire,
That on the ashes of his youth doth lie,
As the death-bed, whereon it must expire,
Consum'd with that which it was nourish'd by.
    This thou perceiv'st, which makes thy love more strong,
    To love that well, which thou must leave ere long.

LXXIV

But be contented: when that fell arrest
Without all bail shall carry me away,
My life hath in this line some interest,
Which for memorial still with thee shall stay.
When thou reviewest this, thou dost review
The very part was consecrate to thee:
The earth can have but earth, which is his due;
My spirit is thine, the better part of me:
So then thou hast but lost the dregs of life,
The prey of worms, my body being dead;
The coward conquest of a wretch's knife,
Too base of thee to be remembered,.
   The worth of that is that which it contains,
   And that is this, and this with thee remains.

LXXV

So are you to my thoughts as food to life,
Or as sweet-season'd showers are to the ground;
And for the peace of you I hold such strife
As 'twixt a miser and his wealth is found.
Now proud as an enjoyer, and anon
Doubting the filching age will steal his treasure;
Now counting best to be with you alone,
Then better'd that the world may see my pleasure:
Sometime all full with feasting on your sight,
And by and by clean starved for a look;
Possessing or pursuing no delight,
Save what is had, or must from you be took.
   Thus do I pine and surfeit day by day,
   Or gluttoning on all, or all away.

LXXVI

Why is my verse so barren of new pride,
So far from variation or quick change?
Why with the time do I not glance aside
To new-found methods, and to compounds strange?
Why write I still all one, ever the same,
And keep invention in a noted weed,
That every word doth almost tell my name,
Showing their birth, and where they did proceed?
O! know sweet love I always write of you,
And you and love are still my argument;
So all my best is dressing old words new,
Spending again what is already spent:
   For as the sun is daily new and old,
   So is my love still telling what is told.

LXXVII

Thy glass will show thee how thy beauties wear,
Thy dial how thy precious minutes waste;
These vacant leaves thy mind's imprint will bear,
And of this book, this learning mayst thou taste.
The wrinkles which thy glass will truly show
Of mouthed graves will give thee memory;
Thou by thy dial's shady stealth mayst know
Time's thievish progress to eternity.
Look! what thy memory cannot contain,
Commit to these waste blanks, and thou shalt find
Those children nursed, deliver'd from thy brain,
To take a new acquaintance of thy mind.
   These offices, so oft as thou wilt look,
   Shall profit thee and much enrich thy book.

LXXVIII

So oft have I invoked thee for my Muse,
And found such fair assistance in my verse
As every alien pen hath got my use
And under thee their poesy disperse.
Thine eyes, that taught the dumb on high to sing
And heavy ignorance aloft to fly,
Have added feathers to the learned's wing
And given grace a double majesty.
Yet be most proud of that which I compile,
Whose influence is thine, and born of thee:
In others' works thou dost but mend the style,
And arts with thy sweet graces graced be;
   But thou art all my art, and dost advance
   As high as learning, my rude ignorance.

LXXIX

Whilst I alone did call upon thy aid,
My verse alone had all thy gentle grace;
But now my gracious numbers are decay'd,
And my sick Muse doth give an other place.
I grant, sweet love, thy lovely argument
Deserves the travail of a worthier pen;
Yet what of thee thy poet doth invent
He robs thee of, and pays it thee again.
He lends thee virtue, and he stole that word
From thy behaviour; beauty doth he give,
And found it in thy cheek: he can afford
No praise to thee, but what in thee doth live.
   Then thank him not for that which he doth say,
   Since what he owes thee, thou thyself dost pay.

LXXX

O! how I faint when I of you do write,
Knowing a better spirit doth use your name,
And in the praise thereof spends all his might,
To make me tongue-tied speaking of your fame!
But since your worth—wide as the ocean is,—
The humble as the proudest sail doth bear,
My saucy bark, inferior far to his,
On your broad main doth wilfully appear.
Your shallowest help will hold me up afloat,
Whilst he upon your soundless deep doth ride;
Or, being wrack'd, I am a worthless boat,
He of tall building, and of goodly pride:
    Then if he thrive and I be cast away,
    The worst was this,—my love was my decay.

LXXXI

Or I shall live your epitaph to make,
Or you survive when I in earth am rotten;
From hence your memory death cannot take,
Although in me each part will be forgotten.
Your name from hence immortal life shall have,
Though I, once gone, to all the world must die:
The earth can yield me but a common grave,
When you entombed in men's eyes shall lie.
Your monument shall be my gentle verse,
Which eyes not yet created shall o'er-read;
And tongues to be, your being shall rehearse,
When all the breathers of this world are dead;
    You still shall live—such virtue hath my pen—
    Where breath most breathes, even in the mouths of men.

LXXXII

I grant thou wert not married to my Muse,
And therefore mayst without attaint o'erlook
The dedicated words which writers use
Of their fair subject, blessing every book.
Thou art as fair in knowledge as in hue,
Finding thy worth a limit past my praise;
And therefore art enforced to seek anew
Some fresher stamp of the time-bettering days.
And do so, love; yet when they have devis'd,
What strained touches rhetoric can lend,
Thou truly fair, wert truly sympathiz'd
In true plain words, by thy true-telling friend;
  And their gross painting might be better us'd
  Where cheeks need blood; in thee it is abus'd.

LXXXIII

I never saw that you did painting need,
And therefore to your fair no painting set;
I found, or thought I found, you did exceed
That barren tender of a poet's debt:
And therefore have I slept in your report,
That you yourself, being extant, well might show
How far a modern[75] quill doth come too short,
Speaking of worth, what worth in you doth grow.
This silence for my sin you did impute,
Which shall be most my glory being dumb;
For I impair not beauty being mute,
When others would give life, and bring a tomb.
  There lives more life in one of your fair eyes
  Than both your poets can in praise devise.

---

[75] Here, as usual in Shakespeare, *modern* is *common, ordinary.*

LXXXIV

Who is it that says most, which can say more,
Than this rich praise,—that you alone, are you?
In whose confine immured is the store
Which should example where your equal grew.
Lean penury within that pen doth dwell
That to his subject lends not some small glory;
But he that writes of you, if he can tell
That you are you, so dignifies his story,
Let him but copy what in you is writ,
Not making worse what nature made so clear,
And such a counterpart shall fame his wit,
Making his style admired every where.
    You to your beauteous blessings add a curse,
    Being fond on praise, which makes your praises worse.

LXXXV

My tongue-tied Muse in manners holds her still,
While comments of your praise richly compiled,
Reserve their character with golden quill,
And precious phrase by all the Muses filed.[76]
I think good thoughts, whilst others write good words,
And like unlettered clerk still cry *Amen*
To every hymn that able spirit affords,
In polish'd form of well-refined pen.
Hearing you praised, I say *'Tis so, 'tis true,*
And to the most of praise add something more;
But that is in my thought, whose love to you,
Though words come hindmost, holds his rank before.
    Then others, for the breath of words respect,
    Me for my dumb thoughts, speaking in effect.

---

[76] *Filed* is *polished* or *finished.* So in Jonson's verses on Shakespeare: "In his well-turned and true-*filed* lines."

LXXXVI

Was it the proud full sail of his great verse,
Bound for the prize of all too precious you,
That did my ripe thoughts in my brain inhearse,
Making their tomb the womb wherein they grew?
Was it his spirit, by spirits taught to write,
Above a mortal pitch, that struck me dead?
No, neither he, nor his compeers by night
Giving him aid, my verse astonished.
He, nor that affable familiar ghost
Which nightly gulls him with intelligence,
As victors of my silence cannot boast;
I was not sick of any fear from thence:
    But when your countenance fill'd up his line,
    Then lacked I matter; that enfeebled mine.

LXXXVII

Farewell! thou art too dear for my possessing,
And like enough thou know'st thy estimate,
The charter of thy worth gives thee releasing;
My bonds in thee are all determinate.
For how do I hold thee but by thy granting?
And for that riches where is my deserving?
The cause of this fair gift in me is wanting,
And so my patent back again is swerving.
Thy self thou gav'st, thy own worth then not knowing,
Or me to whom thou gav'st it, else mistaking;
So thy great gift, upon misprision growing,
Comes home again, on better judgement making.
    Thus have I had thee, as a dream doth flatter,
    In sleep a king, but waking no such matter.

LXXXVIII

When thou shalt be dispos'd to set me light,
And place my merit in the eye of scorn,
Upon thy side, against myself I'll fight,
And prove thee virtuous, though thou art forsworn.
With mine own weakness, being best acquainted,
Upon thy part I can set down a story
Of faults conceal'd, wherein I am attainted;
That thou in losing me shalt win much glory:
And I by this will be a gainer too;
For bending all my loving thoughts on thee,
The injuries that to myself I do,
Doing thee vantage, double-vantage me.
    Such is my love, to thee I so belong,
    That for thy right, myself will bear all wrong.

LXXXIX

Say that thou didst forsake me for some fault,
And I will comment upon that offence:
Speak of my lameness, and I straight will halt,
Against thy reasons making no defence.
Thou canst not love disgrace me half so ill,
To set a form upon desired change,
As I'll myself disgrace; knowing thy will,
I will acquaintance strangle, and look strange;[77]
Be absent from thy walks; and in my tongue
Thy sweet beloved name no more shall dwell,
Lest I, too much profane, should do it wrong,
And haply of our old acquaintance tell.
    For thee, against my self I'll vow debate,[78]
    For I must ne'er love him whom thou dost hate.

---

[77] "I will *smother* my acquaintance, and appear as if I were a *stranger* to you."—
That these words should have been written by Shakespeare!

[78] *Debate*, here, as often, is *contention* or *strife*.

XC

Then hate me when thou wilt; if ever, now;
Now, while the world is bent my deeds to cross,
Join with the spite of fortune, make me bow,
And do not drop in for an after-loss:
Ah! do not, when my heart hath 'scap'd this sorrow,
Come in the rearward of a conquer'd woe;
Give not a windy night a rainy morrow,
To linger out a purpos'd overthrow.
If thou wilt leave me, do not leave me last,
When other petty griefs have done their spite,
But in the onset come: so shall I taste
At first the very worst of fortune's might;
   And other strains of woe, which now seem woe,
   Compar'd with loss of thee, will not seem so.

XCI

Some glory in their birth, some in their skill,
Some in their wealth, some in their body's force,
Some in their garments though new-fangled ill;
Some in their hawks and hounds, some in their horse;
And every humour hath his adjunct pleasure,
Wherein it finds a joy above the rest:
But these particulars are not my measure,
All these I better in one general best.
Thy love is better than high birth to me,
Richer than wealth, prouder than garments' costs,
Of more delight than hawks and horses be;
And having thee, of all men's pride I boast:
   Wretched in this alone, that thou mayst take
   All this away, and me most wretched make.

XCII

But do thy worst to steal thyself away,
For term of life thou art assured mine;
And life no longer than thy love will stay,
For it depends upon that love of thine.
Then need I not to fear the worst of wrongs,
When in the least of them my life hath end.
I see a better state to me belongs
Than that which on thy humour doth depend:
Thou canst not vex me with inconstant mind,
Since that my life on thy revolt doth lie.
O! what a happy title do I find,
Happy to have thy love, happy to die!
   But what's so blessed-fair that fears no blot?
   Thou mayst be false, and yet I know it not.

XCIII

So shall I live, supposing thou art true,
Like a deceived husband; so love's face
May still seem love to me, though alter'd new;
Thy looks with me, thy heart in other place:
For there can live no hatred in thine eye,
Therefore in that I cannot know thy change.
In many's looks, the false heart's history
Is writ in moods, and frowns, and wrinkles strange.
But heaven in thy creation did decree
That in thy face sweet love should ever dwell;
Whate'er thy thoughts, or thy heart's workings be,
Thy looks should nothing thence, but sweetness tell.
   How like Eve's apple doth thy beauty grow,
   If thy sweet virtue answer not thy show!

XCIV

They that have power to hurt, and will do none,
That do not do the thing they most do show,
Who, moving others, are themselves as stone,
Unmoved, cold, and to temptation slow;
They rightly do inherit heaven's graces,
And husband nature's riches from expense;
They are the lords and owners of their faces,
Others, but stewards of their excellence.
The summer's flower is to the summer sweet,
Though to itself, it only live and die,
But if that flower with base infection meet,
The basest weed outbraves his dignity:
   For sweetest things turn sourest by their deeds;
   Lilies that fester, smell far worse than weeds.

XCV

How sweet and lovely dost thou make the shame
Which, like a canker in the fragrant rose,
Doth spot the beauty of thy budding name!
O! in what sweets dost thou thy sins enclose.
That tongue that tells the story of thy days,
Making lascivious comments on thy sport,
Cannot dispraise, but in a kind of praise;
Naming thy name, blesses an ill report.
O! what a mansion have those vices got
Which for their habitation chose out thee,
Where beauty's veil doth cover every blot
And all things turns to fair that eyes can see!
   Take heed, dear heart, of this large privilege;
   The hardest knife ill-us'd doth lose his edge.

XCVI

Some say thy fault is youth, some wantonness;
Some say thy grace is youth and gentle sport;
Both grace and faults are lov'd of more and less:[79]
Thou mak'st faults graces that to thee resort.
As on the finger of a throned queen
The basest jewel will be well esteem'd,
So are those errors that in thee are seen
To truths translated, and for true things deem'd.
How many lambs might the stern wolf betray,
If like a lamb he could his looks translate![80]
How many gazers mightst thou lead away,
if thou wouldst use the strength of all thy state!
   But do not so; I love thee in such sort,
   As, thou being mine, mine is thy good report.

XCVII

How like a winter hath my absence been
From thee, the pleasure of the fleeting year!
What freezings have I felt, what dark days seen!
What old December's bareness everywhere!
And yet this time removed[81] was summer's time;
The teeming autumn, big with rich increase,
Bearing the wanton burden of the prime,
Like widow'd wombs after their lords' decease:
Yet this abundant issue seem'd to me
But hope of orphans, and unfather'd fruit;
For summer and his pleasures wait on thee,
And, thou away, the very birds are mute:
   Or, if they sing, 'tis with so dull a cheer,
   That leaves look pale, dreading the winter's near.

---

[79] "More and less" was a sort of proverbial phrase for "great and small"; that is, all sorts of people. The Poet has it repeatedly.

[80] If he could translate, *change*, his looks into those of a lamb.

[81] "Time *removed*" means time *of remoteness* or *separation*.

XCVIII

From you have I been absent in the spring,
When proud-pied April, dress'd in all his trim,
Hath put a spirit of youth in every thing,
That heavy Saturn laugh'd and leap'd with him.
Yet nor the lays of birds, nor the sweet smell
Of different flowers in odour and in hue,[82]
Could make me any summer's story tell,
Or from their proud lap pluck them where they grew:
Nor did I wonder at the lily's white,
Nor praise the deep vermilion in the rose;
They were but sweet, but figures of delight,
Drawn after you, you pattern of all those.
    Yet seem'd it winter still, and you away,
    As with your shadow I with these did play.

XCIX

The forward violet thus did I chide:
Sweet thief, whence didst thou steal thy sweet that smells,
If not from my love's breath? The purple pride
Which on thy soft cheek for complexion dwells
In my love's veins thou hast too grossly dy'd.
The lily I condemned for thy hand;[83]
And buds of marjoram had stol'n thy hair;
The roses fearfully on thorns did stand,
One blushing shame, another white despair;
A third, nor red nor white, had stol'n of both,
And to his robbery had annex'd thy breath;
But, for his theft, in pride of all his growth
A vengeful canker eat him up to death.
    More flowers I noted, yet I none could see,
    But sweet, or colour it had stol'n from thee.

---

[82] The construction is, "Of flowers different in odour and in hue."
[83] That is, condemned for *stealing the whiteners of* thy hand.

C

Where art thou Muse that thou forget'st so long,
To speak of that which gives thee all thy might?
Spend'st thou thy fury[84] on some worthless song,
Darkening thy power to lend base subjects light?
Return forgetful Muse, and straight redeem,
In gentle numbers time so idly spent;
Sing to the ear that doth thy lays esteem
And gives thy pen both skill and argument.
Rise, resty[85] Muse, my love's sweet face survey,
If Time have any wrinkle graven there;
If any, be a satire to decay,
And make time's spoils despised every where.
 Give my love fame faster than Time wastes life,
 So thou prevent'st his scythe and crooked knife.

---

[84] *Fury* was often thus used for poetic inspiration. So in some verses signed "Hobynoll," written in praise of *The Faerie Queene:*

> Collyn, I see, by thy new-taken taske,
> Some sacred *fury* hath enricht thy braynes,
> That leades thy Muse in haughty verse to maske,
> And loath the layes that 'longs to lowly swaynes;
> That liftes thy notes from Shepheardes unto Kinges:
> So like the lively Larke that mounting singes.

[85] *Resty* is *slothful, dumpish, torpid.* —*Satire,* second line after, is used for *satirist.* So in Ford's *Fancies, Chaste and Noble,* i. 2: "Good! witty rascal, thou'rt a *Satire,* I protest."

CI

O truant Muse what shall be thy amends
For thy neglect of truth in beauty dy'd?
Both truth and beauty on my love depends;
So dost thou too, and therein dignified.
Make answer Muse: wilt thou not haply say,
Truth needs no colour, with his colour fix'd;
Beauty no pencil, beauty's truth to lay;
But best is best, if never intermix'd?
Because he needs no praise, wilt thou be dumb?
Excuse not silence so, for't lies in thee
To make him much outlive a gilded tomb
And to be prais'd of ages yet to be.
   Then do thy office, Muse; I teach thee how
   To make him seem long hence as he shows now.

CII

My love is strengthen'd, though more weak in seeming;
I love not less, though less the show appear;
That love is merchandiz'd, whose rich esteeming,
The owner's tongue doth publish every where.
Our love was new, and then but in the spring,
When I was wont to greet it with my lays;
As Philomel in summer's front doth sing,
And stops her pipe in growth of riper days:
Not that the summer is less pleasant now
Than when her mournful hymns did hush the night,
But that wild music burdens every bough,
And sweets grown common lose their dear delight.
   Therefore like her, I sometime hold my tongue:
   Because I would not dull you with my song.

CIII

Alack! what poverty my Muse brings forth,
That having such a scope to show her pride,
The argument, all bare, is of more worth
Than when it hath my added praise beside!
O! blame me not, if I no more can write!
Look in your glass, and there appears a face
That over-goes my blunt invention quite,
Dulling my lines, and doing me disgrace.
Were it not sinful then, striving to mend,
To mar the subject that before was well?
For to no other pass my verses tend
Than of your graces and your gifts to tell;
    And more, much more, than in my verse can sit,
    Your own glass shows you when you look in it.

CIV

To me, fair friend, you never can be old,
For as you were when first your eye I ey'd,
Such seems your beauty still. Three winters cold,
Have from the forests shook three summers' pride,
Three beauteous springs to yellow autumn turn'd,
In process of the seasons have I seen,
Three April perfumes in three hot Junes burn'd,
Since first I saw you fresh, which yet are green.
Ah! yet doth beauty like a dial-hand,
Steal from his figure, and no pace perceiv'd;
So your sweet hue, which methinks still doth stand,
Hath motion, and mine eye may be deceiv'd:
    For fear of which, hear this thou age unbred:
    Ere you were born was beauty's summer dead.

CV

Let not my love be call'd idolatry,
Nor my beloved as an idol show,
Since all alike my songs and praises be
To one, of one, still such, and ever so.
Kind is my love to-day, to-morrow kind,
Still constant in a wondrous excellence;
Therefore my verse to constancy confin'd,
One thing expressing, leaves out difference.
Fair, kind, and true, is all my argument,—
Fair, kind, and true, varying to other words;
And in this change is my invention spent,
Three themes in one, which wondrous scope affords.
    Fair, kind, and true, have often liv'd alone,
    Which three till now, never kept seat in one.

CVI

When in the chronicle of wasted time
I see descriptions of the fairest wights,
And beauty making beautiful old rime,
In praise of ladies dead and lovely knights,
Then, in the blazon of sweet beauty's best,
Of hand, of foot, of lip, of eye, of brow,
I see their antique pen would have express'd
Even such a beauty as you master now.
So all their praises are but prophecies
Of this our time, all you prefiguring;
And for they looked but with divining eyes,
They had not skill enough your worth to sing:
    For we, which now behold these present days,
    Have eyes to wonder, but lack tongues to praise.

CVII

Not mine own fears, nor the prophetic soul
Of the wide world dreaming on things to come,
Can yet the lease of my true love control,
Supposed as forfeit to a confin'd doom.
The mortal moon hath her eclipse endur'd,
And the sad augurs mock their own presage;
Incertainties now crown themselves assur'd,
And peace proclaims olives of endless age.
Now with the drops of this most balmy time,
My love looks fresh, and Death to me subscribes,[86]
Since, spite of him, I'll live in this poor rime,
While he insults o'er dull and speechless tribes:
    And thou in this shalt find thy monument,
    When tyrants' crests and tombs of brass are spent.

CVIII

What's in the brain, that ink may character,
Which hath not figur'd to thee my true spirit?
What's new to speak, what now to register,
That may express my love, or thy dear merit?
Nothing, sweet boy; but yet, like prayers divine,
I must each day say o'er the very same;
Counting no old thing old, thou mine, I thine,
Even as when first I hallow'd thy fair name.
So that eternal love in love's fresh case,
Weighs not the dust and injury of age,
Nor gives to necessary wrinkles place,
But makes antiquity for aye his page;
    Finding the first conceit of love there bred,
    Where time and outward form would show it dead.

---

[86] *Subscribes* is *resigns, signs away* his prerogative. Often used so by Shakespeare.

CIX

O! never say that I was false of heart,
Though absence seem'd my flame to qualify,
As easy might I from my self depart
As from my soul which in thy breast doth lie:
That is my home of love: if I have rang'd,
Like him that travels, I return again;
Just to the time, not with the time exchang'd,
So that myself bring water for my stain.
Never believe though in my nature reign'd,
All frailties that besiege all kinds of blood,
That it could so preposterously be stain'd,
To leave for nothing all thy sum of good;
   For nothing this wide universe I call,
   Save thou, my rose, in it thou art my all.

CX

Alas! 'tis true, I have gone here and there,
And made my self a motley[87] to the view,
Gor'd mine own thoughts, sold cheap what is most dear,
Made old offences of affections new;
Most true it is, that I have look'd on truth
Askance and strangely; but, by all above,
These blenches[88] gave my heart another youth,
And worse essays prov'd thee my best of love.
Now all is done, save what shall have no end:
Mine appetite I never more will grind
On newer proof, to try an older friend,
A god in love, to whom I am confin'd.
   Then give me welcome, next my heaven the best,
   Even to thy pure and most most loving breast.

---

[87] *Motley,* or *patchwork,* was the proper dress of allowed or professional Fools, and hence the word came to mean *fool.*

[88] To *blench* is to *start* or *fly off from:* so *blenches* here is startings-aside from rectitude. The Poet means, apparently, that lapses have given his heart another youth by proving the strength of his friend's attachment.—Strangely, in the line before, means *as a stranger:* look'd on truth as something *alien* or *foreign* to me. See page 47, note 56.

CXI

O! for my sake do you with Fortune chide,[89]
The guilty goddess of my harmful deeds,
That did not better for my life provide
Than public means which public manners breeds.
Thence comes it that my name receives a brand,
And almost thence my nature is subdu'd
To what it works in, like the dyer's hand:
Pity me, then, and wish I were renew'd;
Whilst, like a willing patient, I will drink,
Potions of eisel[90] 'gainst my strong infection;
No bitterness that I will bitter think,
Nor double penance, to correct correction.
   Pity me then, dear friend, and I assure ye,
   Even that your pity is enough to cure me.[91]

---

[89] To *chide with* means simply to *chide*, that is, *reprove* or *rebuke.*—The construction in the next line is, "The goddess guilty of," &c.

[90] *Eisel* is an old word for *vinegar*; which was thought to be very efficacious as a disinfectant, hence used against contagious diseases.

[91] It is hardly possible to doubt that in the two foregoing Sonnets we have some of the Poet's honest feelings respecting himself. Some foolish rhymester having spoken of Shakespeare and Garrick as kindred minds, Charles Lamb thereupon quotes from these Sonnets, and comments thus: "Who can read these instances of jealous self-watchfulness in our sweet Shakespeare, and dream of any congeniality between him and one that, by every tradition of him, appears to have been as mere a player as ever existed : to have had his mind tainted with the lowest players' vices,—envy and jealousy, and miserable cravings after applause; one who in the exercise of his profession was jealous even of women-performers that stood in his way; a manager full of managerial tricks and stratagems and finesse;—that any resemblance should be dreamed of between him and Shakespeare,—Shakespeare who, in the plenitude and consciousness of his own powers, could, with that noble modesty which we can neither imitate nor appreciate, express himself thus of his own sense of his own defects:

   Wishing me like to one more rich in hope,
   Featured like him, like him with friends possess'd;
   Desiring *this man's art, and that man's scope.*"

CXII

Your love and pity doth the impression fill,
Which vulgar scandal stamp'd upon my brow;
For what care I who calls me well or ill,
So you o'er-green my bad, my good allow?[92]
You are my all-the-world, and I must strive
To know my shames and praises from your tongue;
None else to me, nor I to none alive,That my steel'd sense or
changes right or wrong.[93]
In so profound abysm I throw all care
Of others' voices, that my adder's sense'[94]
To critic and to flatterer stopped are.
Mark how with my neglect I do dispense:
   You are so strongly in my purpose bred,
   That all the world besides methinks are dead.

CXIII

Since I left you, mine eye is in my mind;
And that which governs me to go about
Doth part his function,[95] and is partly blind,
Seems seeing, but effectually is out;
For it no form delivers to the heart
Of bird, of flower, or shape which it doth latch:[96]
Of his quick objects hath the mind no part,
Nor his own vision holds what it doth catch;
For if it see the rud'st or gentlest sight,
The most sweet favour or deformed'st creature,
The mountain or the sea, the day or night:
The crow, or dove, it shapes them to your feature.
   Incapable of more, replete with you,
   My most true mind thus maketh mine untrue.[97]

---

[92] To *allow* is to *approve*, to *hold in esteem*. Generally so in Shakespeare.

[93] Meaning, apparently, "you are the only person that has power to change my hardened *sensibility*, either for the better or for the worse."

[94] Here *sense*' is used as plural. The Poet has other plurals formed in the same way, such as *corpse*', *horse*', *house*'.

[95] In old writers, *part* is not unfrequently equivalent to *depart*, and in that sense is sometimes used transitively, as *depart* is still. So here I take "doth *part* his function" as equivalent to doth *depart from* or *forsake* his function. The context, I think, fairly requires it to be so understood.

[96] To *latch* is to *catch* or *lay hold of*.

CXIV

Or whether doth my mind, being crown'd with you,
Drink up the monarch's plague, this flattery?
Or whether shall I say, mine eye saith true,
And that your love taught it this alchemy,
To make of monsters and things indigest[98]
Such cherubins as your sweet self resemble,
Creating every bad a perfect best,
As fast as objects to his beams assemble?
O! 'tis the first, 'tis flattery in my seeing,
And my great mind most kingly drinks it up:
Mine eye well knows what with his gust is 'greeing,
And to his palate doth prepare the cup:
   If it be poison'd, 'tis the lesser sin
   That mine eye loves it and doth first begin.

CXV

Those lines that I before have writ do lie,
Even those that said I could not love you dearer:
Yet then my judgment knew no reason why
My most full flame should afterwards burn clearer.
But,—reckoning Time, whose million'd accidents
Creep in 'twixt vows, and change decrees of kings,
Tan sacred beauty, blunt the sharp'st intents,
Divert strong minds to the course of altering things;—
Alas! why fearing of Time's tyranny,
Might I not then say, *Now I love you best*,
When I was certain o'er incertainty,
Crowning the present, doubting of the rest?
   Love is a babe, then might I not say so,
   To give full growth to that which still doth grow?

---

[97] *Untrue*, if the text be right, is here used as a. substantive. Malone explains it thus: "The sincerity of my affection is the cause of my untruth, that is, of my not seeing objects truly, such as they appear to the rest of mankind."

[98] *Indigest* is *unformed, shapeless*.

CXVI

Let me not to the marriage of true minds
Admit impediments. Love is not love
Which alters when it alteration finds,
Or bends with the remover to remove:
O, no! it is an ever-fixed mark,
That looks on tempests and is never shaken;[99]
It is the star to every wandering bark,
Whose worth's unknown, although his height be taken.
Love's not Time's fool, though rosy lips and cheeks
Within his bending sickle's compass come;
Love alters not with his brief hours and weeks,
But bears it out even to the edge of doom.
    If this be error and upon me prov'd,
    I never writ, nor no man ever lov'd.

CXVII

Accuse me thus: that I have scanted all,
Wherein I should your great deserts repay,
Forgot upon your dearest love to call,
Whereto all bonds do tie me day by day;
That I have frequent been with unknown minds,
And given to time your own dear-purchas'd right;
That I have hoisted sail to all the winds
Which should transport me farthest from your sight.
Book both my wilfulness and errors down,
And on just proof surmise, accumulate;
Bring me within the level of your frown,
But shoot not at me in your waken'd hate;
    Since my appeal says I did strive to prove
    The constancy and virtue of your love.

---

[99] *Coriolanus*, v. 3, yields an apt comment on this: "And stick i' the wars like a great *sea-mark, standing every flaw,* and saving those that eye thee."

CXVIII

Like as, to make our appetite more keen,
With eager[100] compounds we our palate urge;
As, to prevent our maladies unseen,
We sicken to shun sickness when we purge;
Even so, being full of your ne'er-cloying sweetness,
To bitter sauces did I frame my feeding;
And, sick of welfare, found a kind of meetness
To be diseas'd, ere that there was true needing.
Thus policy in love, t' anticipate
The ills that were not, grew to faults assur'd,
And brought to medicine a healthful state
Which, rank of goodness, would by ill be cur'd;
    But thence I learn and find the lesson true,
    Drugs poison him that so fell sick of you.

CXIX

What potions have I drunk of Siren tears,
Distill'd from limbecks foul as hell within,
Applying fears to hopes, and hopes to fears,
Still losing when I saw myself to win!
What wretched errors hath my heart committed,
Whilst it hath thought itself so blessed never!
How have mine eyes out of their spheres been fitted,[101]
In the distraction of this madding fever!
O benefit of ill! now I find true
That better is, by evil still made better;
And ruin'd love, when it is built anew,
Grows fairer than at first, more strong, far greater.
    So I return rebuk'd to my content,
    And gain by ill thrice more than I have spent.

---

[100] *Eager* is *sharp, acid, biting.*

[101] This, if the text be right, must mean, "How have mine eyes *shot* or *started* from their spheres, *as in a convulsion fit.*" So, in *A Midsummer-Night's Dream*, ii. 1, we have, "And certain stars *shot madly from their spheres.*" Also, in Hamlet, i. 5, "Made thy two eyes, like stars, *start from their spheres.*"

CXX

That you were once unkind befriends me now,
And for that sorrow, which I then did feel,
Needs must I under my transgression bow,
Unless my nerves were brass or hammer'd steel.
For if you were by my unkindness shaken,
As I by yours, you've pass'd a hell of time;
And I, a tyrant, have no leisure taken
To weigh how once I suffer'd in your crime.
O! that our night of woe might have remember'd
My deepest sense,[102] how hard true sorrow hits,
And soon to you, as you to me, then tender'd
The humble salve, which wounded bosoms fits!
   But that your trespass now becomes a fee;
   Mine ransoms yours, and yours must ransom me.

CXXI

'Tis better to be vile than vile esteem'd,
When not to be receives reproach of being;
And the just pleasure lost, which is so deem'd
Not by our feeling, but by others' seeing:
For why should others' false adulterate eyes
Give salutation to my sportive blood?[103]
Or on my frailties why are frailer spies,
Which in their wills count bad what I think good?
No, I am that I am, and they that level[104]
At my abuses reckon up their own:
I may be straight though they themselves be bevel;[105]
By their rank thoughts, my deeds must not be shown;
   Unless this general evil they maintain,
   All men are bad and in their badness reign.

---

[102] *Remember'd* here means *reminded* or *informed*. So in *The Winter's Tale*, iii. 2: "I'll not *remember* you of my own lord." Also, in *King Lear*, i. 4: "Thou but *remember'st* me of mine own conception." And so in divers other places.—"My *deepest sense*" is my *inmost soul*; or, as Hamlet expresses it, "my *heart of heart*."

[103] That is, *flatter* or *exhilarate* my *wanton passions*.

[104] To *level* is a term in gunnery for to *aim*.

[105] *Bevel* is, properly, *slanting, oblique*, or *out of square*.

CXXII

Thy gift, thy tables,[106] are within my brain
Full character'd with lasting memory,
Which shall above that idle rank remain,
Beyond all date; even to eternity:
Or, at the least, so long as brain and heart
Have faculty by nature to subsist;
Till each to raz'd oblivion yield his part
Of thee, thy record never can be miss'd.
That poor retention[107] could not so much hold,
Nor need I tallies thy dear love to score;[108]
Therefore to give them from me was I bold,
To trust those tables that receive thee more:
  To keep an adjunct to remember thee
  Were to import forgetfulness in me.

CXXIII

No, Time, thou shalt not boast that I do change:
Thy pyramids built up with newer might
To me are nothing novel, nothing strange;
They are but dressings of a former sight.
Our dates are brief, and therefore we admire
What thou dost foist upon us that is old;
And rather make them born to our desire
Than think that we before have heard them told.
Thy registers and thee I both defy,
Not wondering at the present nor the past,
For thy records and what we see doth lie,
Made more or less[109] by thy continual haste.
  This I do vow and this shall ever be;
  I will be true despite thy scythe and thee.

---

[106] *Tables,* as the word is here used, were tablets or cards of wax, slate, or ivory, for writing memoranda upon, and were formed into a sort of book, to be carried in the pocket.

[107] Meaning the table-book given him by his friend, and called a "poor retention," because it could hold or retain far less than the living tablets of the mind and heart.

[108] *Tallies* were sticks with which accounts were kept by *scoring* or *cutting notches* in them.

[109] Made *larger* or *smaller*. The meaning is, that Time's record of things is made big or little, to suit his swiftly-changing occasions, and without any regard to what the things are in themselves.

CXXIV

If my dear love were but the child of state,
It might for Fortune's bastard be unfather'd,
As subject to Time's love or to Time's hate,
Weeds among weeds, or flowers with flowers gather'd.
No, it was builded far from accident;
It suffers not in smiling pomp,[110] nor falls
Under the blow of thralled discontent,
Whereto th' inviting time our fashion calls:
It fears not policy, that heretic,
Which works on leases of short-number'd hours,
But all alone stands hugely politic,[111]
That it nor grows with heat, nor drowns with showers.
    To this I witness call the fools of time,
    Which die for goodness, who have lived for crime.[112]

---

[110] "It *suffers* not" means it is not *weakened* or *injured.*

[111] *Hugely politic* is organized or knit together in a huge *polity* or *State.* Rather an odd use of *politic,* to us.

[112] This closing couplet is, to me, exceedingly obscure. The best I can make of it is, "Call on the 'fickle changelings' of time to mark and remember this which I affirm,— those fools who make as if they would die for virtue after having devoted their lives to vice."

CXXV

Were't aught to me I bore the canopy,
With my extern the outward honouring,[113]
Or laid great bases for eternity,
Which proves more short than waste or ruining?
Have I not seen dwellers on form and favour
Lose all and more by paying too much rent
For compound sweet; forgoing simple savour,
Pitiful thrivers, in their gazing spent?
No; let me be obsequious[114] in thy heart,
And take thou my oblation, poor but free,
Which is not mix'd with seconds,[115] knows no art,
But mutual render, only me for thee.
 Hence, thou suborned informer! a true soul
 When most impeach'd, stands least in thy control.

CXXVI

O thou, my lovely boy, who in thy power
Dost hold Time's fickle glass, his sickle-hour;[116]
Who hast by waning grown, and therein show'st
Thy lovers withering, as thy sweet self grow'st.
If Nature, sovereign mistress over wrack,
As thou goest onwards, still will pluck thee back,
She keeps thee to this purpose, that her skill
May time disgrace and wretched minutes kill.
Yet fear her, O thou minion of her pleasure!
She may detain, but not still keep, her treasure:
 Her audit (though delayed) answered must be,
 And her quietus[117] is to render thee.

---

[113] Very obscure, again. Perhaps the meaning is, "Were it of any consequence to me that I walked at the Queen's side, and carried the canopy over her royal head, if I honoured only her outward form with mere external Observances?"

[114] In the 31st *Sonnet* we have "obsequious tear," where *obsequious* is used in an active sense, for *mourning* or *lamenting*. Here it seems to be used in a passive sense, *mourned* or *lamented*.

[115] *Seconds* is a provincial term for the *second kind of flour*, which is collected after the smaller bran is sifted. That our author's oblation was pure, *unmixed with baser matter*, is all that he meant to say.—STEEVENS.

[116] Time's hour, or *course*, is here represented poetically as a sickle, for the same reason that Time is elsewhere figured as being armed with a scythe.— Perhaps it should be noted that here, instead of a sonnet proper, we have a. stanza of twelve lines formed into six couplets.

CXXVII

In the old age black was not counted fair,
Or if it were, it bore not beauty's name;
But now is black beauty's successive heir,
And beauty slander'd with a bastard shame:
For since each hand hath put on Nature's power,
Fairing the foul with Art's false borrowed face,
Sweet beauty hath no name, no holy bower,
But is profan'd, if not lives in disgrace.
Therefore my mistress' eyes are raven black,
Her eyes so suited;[118] and they mourners seem
At such who, not born fair, no beauty lack,
Sland'ring creation with a false esteem:[119]
    Yet so they mourn becoming of their woe,
    That every tongue says beauty should look so.

CXXXIII

How oft when thou, my music, music play'st,
Upon that blessed wood whose motion sounds
With thy sweet fingers when thou gently sway'st
The wiry concord that mine ear confounds,
Do I envy those jacks[120] that nimble leap,
To kiss the tender inward of thy hand,
Whilst my poor lips which should that harvest reap,
At the wood's boldness by thee blushing stand!
To be so tickled, they would change their state
And situation with those dancing chips,
O'er whom thy fingers walk with gentle gait,
Making dead wood more bless'd than living lips.
    Since saucy jacks so happy are in this,
    Give them thy fingers, me thy lips to kiss.

---

[117] *Quietus* in a technical sense,—*discharge, acquittance, release.* So in Webster's *Duchess of Malfi,* iii. 2: "You had the trick in audit-time to be sick, till I had sign'd your *quietus.*"

[118] "Her eyes are so *dressed;*" that is, in *black.*

[119] They seem to mourn, that those who are not born fair are yet possessed of an artificial beauty, by which they pass for what they are not; and thus dishonour nature by their imperfect imitation and false pretensions.—MALONE.

[120] The *jacks* here spoken of are the keys of the virginal upon which the Poet supposes the person addressed to be playing. The verb *envy* often had the accent on the last syllable.

CXXIX

The expense of spirit in a waste of shame
Is lust in action;[121] and till action, lust
Is perjur'd, murderous, bloody, full of blame,
Savage, extreme, rude, cruel, not to trust;
Enjoy'd no sooner but despised straight;
Past reason hunted; and no sooner had,
Past reason hated, as a swallow'd bait,
On purpose laid to make the taker mad:
Mad in pursuit and in possession so;
Had, having, and in quest, to have extreme;
A bliss in proof,—and prov'd, a very woe;
Before, a joy propos'd; behind a dream.
    All this the world well knows; yet none knows well
    To shun the heaven that leads men to this hell.

CXXX

My mistress' eyes are nothing like the sun;
Coral is far more red, than her lips red:
If snow be white, why then her breasts are dun;
If hairs be wires, black wires grow on her head.
I have seen roses damask'd, red and white,
But no such roses see I in her cheeks;
And in some perfumes is there more delight
Than in the breath that from my mistress reeks.
I love to hear her speak,—yet well I know
That music hath a far more pleasing sound:
I grant I never saw a goddess go,—
My mistress, when she walks, treads on the ground:
    And yet by heaven, I think my love as rare,
    As any she belied with false compare.

---

[121] The construction is, "Lust in action is th' expense of spirit," &c.

CXXXI

Thou art as tyrannous, so as thou art,
As those whose beauties proudly make them cruel;
For well thou know'st to my dear doting heart
Thou art the fairest and most precious jewel.
Yet, in good faith, some say that thee behold,
Thy face hath not the power to make love groan;
To say they err I dare not be so bold,
Although I swear it to myself alone.
And to be sure that is not false I swear,
A thousand groans, but thinking on thy face,
One on another's neck, do witness bear
Thy black is fairest in my judgment's place.
   In nothing art thou black save in thy deeds,
   And thence this slander, as I think, proceeds.

CXXXII

Thine eyes I love, and they, as pitying me,
Knowing thy heart torment me with disdain,
Have put on black and loving mourners be,
Looking with pretty ruth upon my pain.
And truly not the morning sun of heaven
Better becomes the grey cheeks of the east,
Nor that full star that ushers in the even,
Doth half that glory to the sober west,
As those two mourning eyes become thy face:
O! let it then as well beseem thy heart
To mourn for me since mourning doth thee grace,
And suit thy pity like in every part.
   Then will I swear beauty herself is black,
   And all they foul that thy complexion lack.

CXXXIII

Beshrew that heart that makes my heart to groan
For that deep wound it gives my friend and me!
Is't not enough to torture me alone,
But slave to slavery my sweet'st friend must be?
Me from myself thy cruel eye hath taken,
And my next self thou harder hast engross'd:
Of him, myself, and thee I am forsaken;
A torment thrice three-fold thus to be cross'd:
Prison my heart in thy steel bosom's ward,
But then my friend's heart let my poor heart bail;
Whoe'er keeps me,[122] let my heart be his guard;
Thou canst not then use rigour in my jail:
    And yet thou wilt; for I, being pent in thee,
    Perforce am thine, and all that is in me.

CXXXIV

So, now I have confess'd that he is thine,
And I my self am mortgag'd to thy will,
Myself I'll forfeit, so that other mine
Thou wilt restore to be my comfort still:
But thou wilt not, nor he will not be free,
For thou art covetous, and he is kind;
He learn'd but surety-like to write for me,
Under that bond that him as fast doth bind.
The statute[123] of thy beauty thou wilt take,
Thou usurer, that putt'st forth all to use,
And sue a friend came debtor for my sake;
So him I lose through my unkind abuse.
    Him have I lost; thou hast both him and me:
    He pays the whole, and yet am I not free.

---

[122] "*Keeps* me" is *guards* or *defends* me. To *keep* was often so used.

[123] *Statute* has here its legal signification, that of a security or obligation for money.—MALONE.

CXXXV

Whoever hath her wish, thou hast thy *Will*.[124]
And *Will* to boot, and *Will* in over-plus;
More than enough am I that vex'd thee still,
To thy sweet will making addition thus.
Wilt thou, whose will is large and spacious,
Not once vouchsafe to hide my will in thine?
Shall will in others seem right gracious,
And in my will no fair acceptance shine?
The sea, all water, yet receives rain still,
And in abundance addeth to his store;
So thou, being rich in *Will*, add to thy *Will*
One will of mine, to make thy large *Will* more.
   Let no unkind no fair beseechers kill;
   Think all but one, and me in that one *Will*.

CXXXVI

If thy soul check thee that I come so near,
Swear to thy blind soul that I was thy *Will*,
And will, thy soul knows, is admitted there;
Thus far for love, my love-suit, sweet, fulfil.
Will, will fulfil the treasure of thy love,
Ay, fill it full with wills, and my will one.
In things of great receipt with ease we prove
Among a number one is reckon'd none:[125]
Then in the number let me pass untold,
Though in thy store's account I one must be;
For nothing hold me, so it please thee hold
That nothing me, a something sweet to thee:
   Make but my name thy love, and love that still,
   And then thou lov'st me,—for my name is *Will*.

---

[124] The play upon *Will* in this Sonnet and the next evidently refers to the Poet's own name.

[125] Several allusions have been found to this way of reckoning.

CXXXVII

Thou blind fool, Love, what dost thou to mine eyes,
That they behold, and see not what they see?
They know what beauty is, see where it lies,
Yet what the best is take the worst to be.
If eyes, corrupt by over-partial looks,
Be anchor'd in the bay where all men ride,
Why of eyes' falsehood hast thou forged hooks,
Whereto the judgment of my heart is tied?
Why should my heart think that a several plot,
Which my heart knows the wide world's common place?[126]
Or mine eyes, seeing this, say this is not,
To put fair truth upon so foul a face?
    In things right true my heart and eyes have err'd,
    And to this false plague are they now transferr'd.

CXXXVIII

When my love swears that she is made of truth,
I do believe her though I know she lies,
That she might think me some untutor'd youth,
Unlearned in the world's false subtleties.
Thus vainly thinking that she thinks me young,
Although she knows my days are past the best,
Simply I credit her false-speaking tongue:
On both sides thus is simple truth suppressed:
But wherefore says she not she is unjust?
And wherefore say not I that I am old?
O! love's best habit is in seeming trust,
And age in love, loves not to have years told:
    Therefore I lie with her, and she with me,
    And in our faults by lies we flatter'd be.

---

[126] "A several plot," as distinguished from a "common place," is a piece of ground that has been separated and made private property. A similar play upon *several* and *common* occurs in *Love's Labours Lost*.

CXXXIX

O! call not me to justify the wrong
That thy unkindness lays upon my heart;
Wound me not with thine eye, but with thy tongue:
Use power with power, and slay me not by art,
Tell me thou lov'st elsewhere; but in my sight,
Dear heart, forbear to glance thine eye aside:
What need'st thou wound with cunning, when thy might
Is more than my o'erpress'd defence can bide?
Let me excuse thee: ah! my love well knows
Her pretty looks have been mine enemies;
And therefore from my face she turns my foes,
That they elsewhere might dart their injuries:
    Yet do not so; but since I am near slain,
    Kill me outright with looks, and rid my pain.

CXL

Be wise as thou art cruel; do not press
My tongue-tied patience with too much disdain;
Lest sorrow lend me words, and words express
The manner of my pity-wanting pain.
If I might teach thee wit, better it were,
Though not to love, yet, love to tell me so;—
As testy sick men, when their deaths be near,
No news but health from their physicians know;—
For, if I should despair, I should grow mad,
And in my madness might speak ill of thee;
Now this ill-wresting world is grown so bad,
Mad slanderers by mad ears believed be.
    That I may not be so, nor thou belied,
    Bear thine eyes straight, though thy proud heart go wide.

CXLI

In faith I do not love thee with mine eyes,
For they in thee a thousand errors note;
But 'tis my heart that loves what they despise,
Who, in despite of view, is pleased to dote.
Nor are mine ears with thy tongue's tune delighted;
Nor tender feeling, to base touches prone,
Nor taste, nor smell, desire to be invited
To any sensual feast with thee alone:
But my five wits[127] nor my five senses can
Dissuade one foolish heart from serving thee,
Who leaves unsway'd the likeness of a man,
Thy proud heart's slave and vassal wretch to be:
   Only my plague thus far I count my gain,
   That she that makes me sin awards me pain.

CXLII

Love is my sin, and thy dear virtue hate,
Hate of my sin, grounded on sinful loving:
O! but with mine compare thou thine own state,
And thou shalt find it merits not reproving;
Or, if it do, not from those lips of thine,
That have profan'd their scarlet ornaments
And seal'd false bonds of love as oft as mine,
Robb'd others' beds' revenues of their rents.
Be it lawful I love thee, as thou lov'st those
Whom thine eyes woo as mine importune thee:
Root pity in thy heart, that, when it grows,
Thy pity may deserve to pitied be.
   If thou dost seek to have what thou dost hide,
   By self-example mayst thou be denied!

---

[127] The *wits* are the intellectual faculties, which were supposed to correspond in number with the senses.

CXLIII

Lo, as a careful housewife runs to catch
One of her feather'd creatures broke away,
Sets down her babe, and makes all swift dispatch
In pursuit of the thing she would have stay;
Whilst her neglected child holds her in chase,
Cries to catch her whose busy care is bent
To follow that which flies before her face,
Not prizing her poor infant's discontent;
So runn'st thou after that which flies from thee,
Whilst I thy babe chase thee afar behind;
But if thou catch thy hope, turn back to me,
And play the mother's part, kiss me, be kind;
   So will I pray that thou mayst have thy *Will*,
   If thou turn back and my loud crying still.

CXLIV

Two loves I have of comfort and despair,
Which like two spirits do suggest[128] me still:
The better angel is a man right fair,
The worser spirit a woman colour'd ill.
To win me soon to hell, my female evil,
Tempteth my better angel from my side,
And would corrupt my saint to be a devil,
Wooing his purity with her foul pride.
And whether that my angel be turn'd fiend,
Suspect I may, yet not directly tell;
But being both from me, both to each friend,
I guess one angel in another's hell:
   Yet this shall I ne'er know, but live in doubt,
   Till my bad angel fire my good one out.

---

[128] Here, as usual, to *suggest* is to *tempt* or *incite*.

CXLV

Those lips that Love's own hand did make,
Breathed forth the sound that said *I hate*
To me that languish'd for her sake:
But when she saw my woeful state,
Straight in her heart did mercy come,
Chiding that tongue that ever sweet
Was us'd in giving gentle doom;
And taught it thus anew to greet;
I hate she alter'd with an end,
That followed it as gentle day,
Doth follow night, who like a fiend
From heaven to hell is flown away.
    I hate from hate away she threw,
    And sav'd my life, saying—*Not you.*

CXLVI

Poor soul, the centre of my sinful earth,
My sinful earth these rebel powers aray,[129]
Why dost thou pine within and suffer dearth,
Painting thy outward walls so costly gay?
Why so large cost, having so short a lease,
Dost thou upon thy fading mansion spend?
Shall worms, inheritors of this excess,
Eat up thy charge? Is this thy body's end?
Then soul, live thou upon thy servant's loss,
And let that pine to aggravate thy store;
Buy terms[130] divine in selling hours of dross;
Within be fed, without be rich no more:
    So shall thou feed on Death, that feeds on men,
    And Death once dead, there's no more dying then.

---

[129] *Aray* is an old word meaning to *affict*, to *ill-treat*, to *bring to an evil condition.* So in Horman's *Vulgaria*, 1530, quoted by Dyce: "He was sore *arayed* with sycknesse. Morbo atrociter *conflictus est.*" Also, in *Reynard the Fox*, 1481, when Isegrim the wolf has received a kick on the head from a mare, he says to Reynard, "I am so foule *arayed* and sore hurte, that an herte of stone might have pyte of me." And in *Paris and Vienna*, 1459, quoted by Ingleby: "And on the morrowe erly the ten men of armes came tofore the daulphyn alle wounded and sore hurte. And they recounted to hym how two yonge men onely had *arayed* them so, and how they nedes must flee for fere of theyr lyves." And so the meaning in the text appears to be, that the "sinful earth," that is, the lusts of the flesh, conspires or joins with the external temptations, the "rebel powers," which "assault and hurt the soul"; the two together causing it to "pine within and suffer dearth."

[130] *Terms* in the legal and academic sense; that is, long periods of time as opposed to hours. —*Aggravate* in the sense of *increase*.

CXLVII

My love is as a fever longing still,
For that which longer nurseth the disease;
Feeding on that which doth preserve the ill,
The uncertain sickly appetite to please.
My reason, the physician to my love,
Angry that his prescriptions are not kept,
Hath left me, and I desperate now approve
Desire is death, which physic did except.
Past cure I am, now Reason is past care,
And frantic-mad with evermore unrest;
My thoughts and my discourse as madmen's are,
At random from the truth vainly express'd;
    For I have sworn thee fair, and thought thee bright,
    Who art as black as hell, as dark as night.

CXLVIII

O me! what eyes hath Love put in my head,
Which have no correspondence with true sight;
Or, if they have, where is my judgment fled,
That censures falsely[131] what they see aright?
If that be fair whereon my false eyes dote,
What means the world to say it is not so?
If it be not, then love doth well denote
Love's eye[132] is not so true as all men's: no,
How can it? O! how can Love's eye be true,
That is so vexed with watching and with tears?
No marvel then, though I mistake my view;
The sun itself sees not, till heaven clears.
    O cunning Love! with tears thou keep'st me blind,
    Lest eyes well-seeing thy foul faults should find.

---

[131] That *judges* or *estimates* falsely. So *censure* was commonly used.
[132] A quibble between *eye* and *ay*, which appear to have been pronounced alike.

CXLIX

Canst thou, O cruel! say I love thee not,
When I against myself with thee partake?[133]
Do I not think on thee, when I forgot
Am of my self, all tyrant, for thy sake?
Who hateth thee that I do call my friend,
On whom frown'st thou that I do fawn upon,
Nay, if thou lour'st on me, do I not spend
Revenge upon myself with present moan?
What merit do I in my self respect,
That is so proud thy service to despise,
When all my best doth worship thy defect,
Commanded by the motion of thine eyes?
 But, love, hate on, for now I know thy mind;
 Those that can see thou lov'st, and I am blind.

CL

O! from what power hast thou this powerful might,
With insufficiency my heart to sway?
To make me give the lie to my true sight,
And swear that brightness doth not grace the day?
Whence hast thou this becoming of things ill,[134]
That in the very refuse of thy deeds
There is such strength and warrantise of skill,
That, in my mind, thy worst all best exceeds?
Who taught thee how to make me love thee more,
The more I hear and see just cause of hate?
O! though I love what others do abhor,
With others thou shouldst not abhor my state:
 If thy unworthiness rais'd love in me,
 More worthy I to be belov'd of thee.

---

[133] *Partake* is here equivalent to *take part.*
[134] That is, this *power of adorning* things ill, or making them appear beautiful.

CLI

Love is too young to know what conscience is,
Yet who knows not conscience is born of love?
Then, gentle cheater, urge not my amiss,[135]
Lest guilty of my faults thy sweet self prove:
For, thou betraying me, I do betray
My nobler part to my gross body's treason;
My soul doth tell my body that he may
Triumph in love; flesh stays no farther reason,
But rising at thy name doth point out thee,
As his triumphant prize. Proud of this pride,
He is contented thy poor drudge to be,
To stand in thy affairs, fall by thy side.
   No want of conscience hold it that I call
   Her *love*, for whose dear love I rise and fall.

CLII

In loving thee thou know'st I am forsworn,
But thou art twice forsworn, to me love swearing;
In act thy bed-vow broke, and new faith torn,
In vowing new hate after new love bearing:
But why of two oaths' breach do I accuse thee,
When I break twenty? I am perjur'd most;
For all my vows are oaths but to misuse thee,
And all my honest faith in thee is lost:
For I have sworn deep oaths of thy deep kindness,
Oaths of thy love, thy truth, thy constancy;
And, to enlighten thee, gave eyes to blindness,
Or made them swear against the thing they see;
   For I have sworn thee fair,—more perjur'd I,
   To swear against the truth so foul a lie.

---

[135] *Amiss* again as a substantive. See page 38, note 36.—*Cheater* here means *escheator*, an officer of the Exchequer.

CLIII

Cupid laid by his brand and fell asleep:
A maid of Dian's this advantage found,
And his love-kindling fire did quickly steep
In a cold valley-fountain of that ground;
Which borrow'd from this holy fire of Love,
A dateless lively heat, still to endure,
And grew a seething bath, which yet men prove
Against strange maladies a sovereign cure.
But at my mistress' eye Love's brand new-fired,
The boy for trial needs would touch my breast;
I, sick withal, the help of bath desired,
And thither hied, a sad distemper'd guest,
   But found no cure, the bath for my help lies
   Where Cupid got new fire,—my mistress' eyes.

CLIV

The little Love-god lying once asleep,
Laid by his side his heart-inflaming brand,
Whilst many nymphs that vow'd chaste life to keep
Came tripping by; but in her maiden hand
The fairest votary took up that fire
Which many legions of true hearts had warm'd;
And so the general of hot desire
Was, sleeping, by a virgin hand disarm'd.
This brand she quenched in a cool well by,
Which from Love's fire took heat perpetual,
Growing a bath and healthful remedy,
For men diseas'd; but I, my mistress' thrall,
   Came there for cure and this by that I prove,
   Love's fire heats water, water cools not love.[136]

THE END

---

[136] On these last two Sonnets Malone notes as follows: "They seem to have been early essays of the Poet, who perhaps had not determined which of them he should prefer. He could hardly have intended to send them both into the world."